T0322093

MEDITATION
for the REAL WORLD

MEDITATION
for the REAL WORLD

Finding peace in everyday life

Ann Swanson

CONTENTS

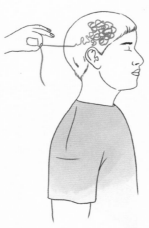

02

03

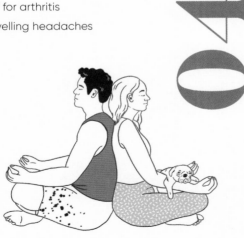

Foreword

Thirty years ago, I developed a sports injury and went to a yoga class on the advice of a physical therapist. At that time, few people did yoga or meditation, and it was still widely viewed as a strange, esoteric practice by most people.

The yoga classes always ended with 10 minutes of meditation. At first, I was resistant to this practice and would just sit there and think about my to-do list rather than follow the teacher's instructions. Then one day I decided to give it a try, and I noticed how just those 10 minutes could impact my mood and sense of calm. Over several weeks I started noticing how I was becoming more calm in general, more in touch with my emotions, and better able to tune in to what others were saying.

I was intrigued about how meditation could produce such profound results, and so I decided to focus my research career on trying to understand how meditation works scientifically. Over the past 25 years there has been an explosion of research around the globe demonstrating the many benefits of meditation on physical and mental health, as well as its impact on concentration,

mental clarity, memory, and complex cognitive tasks. The research also demonstrates how meditation can boost emotional wellbeing and enhance the quality of our relationships. In this book we demystify these ancient practices and share the most relevant research with you so you can apply it to your life.

Most books about meditation focus on establishing a formal meditation practice where you sit still and focus your breath for 30–60 minutes per day. Our goal with this book is to highlight all the different ways meditation techniques can be applied to help you navigate the modern world. Ann offers numerous short meditation practices that can be strategically sprinkled throughout your day, and provides skilful suggestions for weaving mindfulness and meditation techniques into your daily activities.

I find that these short, targeted meditation practices can provide big benefits, and I hope you do, too.

Dr Sara Lazar
Meditation and yoga researcher, Harvard Medical School and Massachusetts General Hospital

From ancient wisdom to apps and AI

Do you find the idea of meditation intimidating? Do you think your mind wanders too much, so you give up? Do you ever feel like you don't have time to meditate? I hope this book of real-world meditations will change your mind (both figuratively and literally).

Listen, I'm no guru. I am not a monk or a nun, nor have I ever been. I'm not a celebrity or even an influencer. I'm just a regular person who deals with sporadic social anxiety, chronic joint pain since I was a teenager, a fear of medical procedures that is so bad I pass out, and other real-world problems. Now, I'm a meditation teacher, but I wasn't naturally a "chill" person. Meditation seems quite simple, but consistent practice didn't come easily to me – at my first meditation retreat, when I was 19, my friend and I broke our vow of silence and then escaped into the night!

Long retreats or unsustainable homework to sit in silence for an hour a day felt intimidating to start with, but since my retreat escapade, I've often turned to meditation techniques to navigate everyday challenges. Burnout, binge-watching, imposter syndrome, and mindless scrolling are modern manifestations of ancient problems. And if ancient people felt that meditation was needed to address suffering, nowadays we need it more than ever.

The good news is that modern technology provides us with guided meditations at our fingertips – or by voice activation. Just now, I said out loud: "Alexa, do you meditate?" Apparently, even she knows how, and she suggested methods to help me relax. This practice has stood the test of time and served so many for a reason: meditation works.

The side effects of meditation may include creativity, productivity, and clarity. But meditation promises something even more profound with practice. Meditation was developed to lead to a higher state of liberation, which some call enlightenment or union with the divine. I went through a dark period when I struggled to get out of bed during the day and couldn't sleep at night due to racing thoughts. I did something simple, which made a profound difference. I kicked the habit of automatically pressing the Gmail or Instagram icons on my phone, by moving multiple meditation apps to the homepage.

One relaxing 10-minute meditation turned into another. Hits of dopamine and serotonin kept me reopening the apps as I felt my mood and mindset improve. I felt lighter during a heavy time. This was when I began my "meditation marathons". Just as we can fall into self-destructive and unhealthy patterns, we can also get into health-promoting cycles, and starting small initiates that momentum. I soon found myself naturally meditating the recommended hour per day and infusing mindfulness into simple activities like washing the dishes.

For the past two decades, neuroscientist Dr Sara Lazar and her team at Harvard have been peering into the brains of meditators to uncover how it works. Dr Lazar's groundbreaking research suggests that meditation can help protect the brain from typical age-related decline – and that as little as eight weeks of practice can literally change your brain. Her recent research on compassion and empathy illuminates meditation's potential for enhancing mental health and wellbeing, too. I'm grateful to have Dr Lazar advising on the cutting-edge neuroscience explored in this book. You'll find the citations for each claim on page 181.

This isn't another self-help book; it's a self-compassion book for befriending your mind. It is a practical, how-to guide for navigating real-world situations, such as social awkwardness, test anxiety, and family gatherings, using simple meditation practices. Through trying these practical techniques while you read, which give immediate benefits, I hope you'll find yourself meditating more. Maybe one day, you'll get through a challenging time with meditation marathons, too.

Ann Swanson
MS in Yoga Therapy, LMT,
C-IAYT, ERYT500

CHAPTER 1

HOW MEDITATION WORKS

Ask yourself an important question: why practise meditation? Why did you pick up this book? Are you looking for relaxation, relief from anxiety or pain, improved productivity, better sleep, or perhaps something even more profound? Meditation can offer all these benefits and more, helping you become the person you aspire to be.

In this chapter, we will explore what meditation is, who meditates, when is best, and where to practise. We will also discover why meditation could be the most important skill you ever learn to help you navigate the real world and connect more deeply to yourself and others.

Consider this a user-friendly guide on how to practise and an overview on how meditation works – based on science. There are now thousands of studies illuminating the health benefits of meditation, so in these pages, you'll also uncover the research behind the practice. We'll start with the most frequently asked questions about meditation.

What is meditation?

Meditation is the practice of focusing your attention and awareness on the present moment in a relaxed way, to promote clarity and emotional stability. With meditation, you are cultivating a state of mind that is easeful, open, curious, accepting, compassionate, and kind – to yourself and others.

Meditation involves a different kind of focus to the one you're used to in everyday life. Your mind likely approaches work projects and other goal-oriented tasks by analysing, evaluating, and judging in order to achieve a specific outcome. Meditation involves a softer kind of focus through a nurturing lens, without pressure to win or succeed.

Contrary to what many think, this process isn't about getting rid of your problems and being at peace all the time. It isn't just for monks in a monastery or temple. It is something far more grounded in the practical, everyday world. This book uses specific meditation techniques alongside other therapeutic tools and lifestyle tips to help you navigate real-life situations.

Meditation shifts your perspective on the world and your relationship with your *self*. It allows you to take a break from the daily grind and sit with your thoughts, observing them in a concentrated, caring way. It trains you to manage your attention and direct it to what is, rather than what might be. You may choose to focus on your breath, the sounds around you, or the ground beneath your feet. Attention with intention is a skill that comes with practice. Like reading, meditation is something you learn, not something you are born with. It is often described as a form of exercise for your brain, with benefits expanding beyond your body to your life – from improving relationships to opening your awareness to new possibilities.

Meditation is a form of exercise for your brain.

How do I practise meditation?

You may imagine you need to sit on the floor with your legs crossed for an hour every morning to call yourself a meditator, but practising meditation is not what you think. There is no one "right" way to meditate. It is infinitely customizable, making it accessible and practical – even in modern life. You can meditate on the floor, at a desk, as you walk, on a bus, in bed to wind down, or nearly anywhere at anytime. Ultimately, the best method is the one you enjoy and that fits into your unique lifestyle.

Is it religious?

You don't have to be in any specific religion to meditate. Meditation is an inclusive practice. Anyone of any religion or perspective can enjoy the benefits. Historically, meditation has an association with many religions and philosophical traditions, mainly Hinduism and Buddhism, as well as Taoism and Jainism. Meditative practices can be identified in other religions too, including chanting and specific types of prayer in Christianity and Judaism, and mindful movement is incorporated into Islamic prayer. In the 1970s, Western researchers (including Jon Kabat-Zinn and Herbert Benson) realized that meditation could be practised in a secular way, which showed beneficial changes in physiology along with decreased stress and pain.

Is it spiritual?

Meditation can be spiritual or not. "Spiritual" means different things to different people. Some define spirituality as a connection to a higher power (as part of a religion or not). Others describe spirituality as feeling in union with nature, and meditation certainly helps us to connect with our natural environment (see page 153) and recognize our true nature. What is clear is that meditation can be truly transformational. It is quite common to hear, "Meditation changed my life," or even, "Meditation saved my life." The practice can lead to profound shifts in life perspective, bringing deeper meaning and purpose.

Meditation can lead to profound shifts in life perspective.

Meditation is about stopping your thoughts

Many people think that meditating is about stopping thoughts completely, but it isn't. In many forms of meditation, you simply observe thoughts arising and disappearing. It's like watching clouds or bubbles pass by while remaining aware of the vast, clear blue sky in which they float. It is entirely natural to get carried away by thoughts, getting into a mental conversation about the past or future.

In fact, this capacity to mentally "time travel" is what some propose makes us uniquely human; our prefrontal cortex gives us this ability to analyse and plan, and ours is proportionally larger than that of most other species. (For more on how the brain works during meditation, see page 38.)

Don't be concerned with natural mind-wandering. Even the most advanced meditator experiences this, though it happens less frequently the more you practise. It doesn't mean you are bad at meditating. Instead, see it as an opportunity to practise returning to the present. Rather than trying to master or control your mind, you can think of it as befriending your mind.

What are the different meditation techniques?

Meditation is a group of traditions and practices from all over the world, with historians dating it back thousands of years. There are many types of meditation, and they incorporate lots of different techniques – more than can be listed here!

Some meditation techniques ask you to focus on one thing that you do or experience externally, like a word you repeat (mantra), a candle flame you stare at, or a sound you intently listen to. Others invite you to observe an internal experience, like the flow of your thoughts or physical sensations. Different techniques have varying effects, and one of the most popular is mindfulness.

What is mindfulness?

Mindfulness is the practice of being intentionally present with whatever is happening, including being aware of internal states and surroundings. Rather than analysing or judging (as our minds are often trained to do), we gently redirect our focus to simply observe whatever arises, including thoughts, emotions, physical sensations, breathing, sounds, or any other element of the present experience.

You can be mindful at any time, under any circumstances – from eating to brushing your teeth. However, it is hard to remember to be mindful when life gets stressful. A formal mindfulness meditation practice can strengthen the skill of everyday mindfulness, just as practising an instrument increases skill and quality in a concert. It involves setting aside time to focus on an object of attention in the present moment, such as the breath. When the mind naturally wanders, the focus is directed back to that object with self-compassion.

The popularity of mindfulness stems from its accessibility to beginners and its extensive use in research, including mindfulness-based stress reduction (MBSR). Modern mindfulness is largely derived from Vipassana meditation, or "insight meditation", which seeks insight into the true nature of reality.

Mindfulness programmes also incorporate philosophies from Zen (a cut-to-the chase type of Buddhism and meditation). MBSR also incorporates practices with Hindu roots such as yoga, but does so in a secular way. Discover some of the many different ways to meditate, which include mindfulness and beyond, in the chart below. Then figure out which ones work best for you.

You have many options to try!

Here are just some of the many ways you can meditate and we will be looking at all of them in the book.

Breath awareness: *focuses on breath to anchor you to the present.*	**Breathing exercises:** *also called breathwork in the West and pranayama in yoga.*	**Body awareness:** *focuses on body sensations.*
Body scan: *systematically moves attention through the body.*	**Chakra meditation:** *focuses on energy centres in the body, including the third eye.*	**Labelling or noting:** *categorizing thoughts.*
Loving-kindness (metta): *cultivates compassion for yourself and others.*	**Mantra:** *repeating a word, phrase, or sound (like "om").*	**Mindful movement:** *includes yoga, tai chi, qi gong, dance, and walking meditation.*
Mudra: *creates intentional shapes with the body or hands.*	**Open awareness or open monitoring:** *observing broad, changing experiences.*	**Progressive muscle relaxation:** *squeezing and releasing muscles.*
Reflection: *contemplates a specific topic or question.*	**Sound:** *involves listening to or making sounds.*	**Tonglen:** *a Tibetan technique of sending and receiving.*
Visualization: *envisioning a scene or scenario.*		**Yoga nidra:** *a sleep-like deep relaxation practice.*

How do we benefit from meditation?

Meditation was initially developed to alleviate suffering and reach enlightenment. Today, it is used to ease pain, improve mood, optimize focus and performance, and support overall wellbeing.

The techniques in this book will guide you to fit meditation into your daily routine and build them into a regular practice so you can experience the real-world benefits for yourself. Here are some of the ways meditation can enhance your life.

Mood regulation: Meditation helps alleviate anxiety and depression symptoms and boosts feelings of happiness and compassion.

Stress resilience: Meditation helps to regulate your nervous system during high-pressure moments.

Pain relief: Meditation eases chronic pain such as arthritis, so you can do the activities you enjoy.

Healthy heart: Meditation improves cardiovascular health in many ways, including lowering blood pressure and slowing your heart rate.

Less inflammation: Meditation reduces blood inflammatory markers and calms activity in inflammation-related genes, which could ease disease symptoms and help prevent illnesses.

Immunity: Meditation improves your immune system's ability to fight invading bacteria and viruses, which could help prevent you from getting sick. And when you are sick meditation can help you recover.

Addiction recovery: Meditation is associated with making better lifestyle choices, which could prevent drug abuse and support addiction recovery.

Focus, cognition, and memory: Meditation improves attention regulation, problem-solving, and working memory.

Performance: A side effect of meditation is better work and sports performance – often beyond what people imagine.

Creativity: Meditation enhances creative thinking and problem-solving.

Am I already meditating?

Meditation is a specific way of focusing, but some other activities reach similar (though not identical) brain states and levels of concentration.

You may be wondering: is prayer meditation? How about hypnosis? What about when I am in flow playing a musical instrument? All of these activities have meditative elements, even though they are not strictly meditation themselves.

Flow state

Numerous other activities besides meditation can put you in an extreme state of focus, which psychologists call "flow" – what we colloquially call being "in the zone". This is a mental state where you are completely absorbed in what you are doing, whether that is playing the piano, creating a work of art, or organizing your cabinets. Both flow state and meditation shift brainwaves from beta, which are associated with thinking and conversing, to mostly alpha and theta, which are related to relaxing and creativity. Meditation could be considered a type of flow state, but not all flow states are meditation. Distinct regions of the brain are activated when you are in flow while dancing, for example, compared to when you are sitting and meditating. Being in a flow state is therefore better described as mindful or meditative, rather than meditation.

Prayer

Prayer is similar to meditation in many ways, but it also activates different parts of your brain. One way to think of it is that prayer is a way to talk to God or a higher power, and meditation is the practice of listening. An emerging field of research, neurotheology, is uncovering the power of prayer, and how it differs from meditation. For example, neuroscience researcher Dr Andrew B. Newberg says that when praying, brain activity is similar to when we're talking to someone. When meditating, brain activity can be closer to visualization, activating the areas of the brain responsible for processing visual input.

Hypnosis

A hypnosis experience involves focused attention (like meditation) and a tendency to be immediately responsive to suggestions of actions to take (unlike meditation). During meditation you are highly aware (and aware of being aware); in contrast, during hypnosis, you are not always fully aware. Some self-hypnosis protocols incorporate meditation techniques and some types of meditation have been described as having hypnotic qualities, but, despite this overlap, hypnosis is not meditation.

Non-sleep deep rest

Google CEO Sundar Pichai finds it difficult to do a traditional seated meditation, so he practises non-sleep deep rest (NSDR) instead to help him recover from lost sleep and to improve his focus. NSDR is a term coined by Stanford neuroscientist Dr Andrew D. Huberman. It is a sleep-like state, characterized by brainwaves associated with deep relaxation and sleep (see page 40), achieved through a guided meditation called yoga nidra and some types of hypnosis. In many cases, when someone says they are practising an NSDR, they are practising yoga nidra, which means "yogic sleep" and is typically practised lying down for 20 minutes or more to induce deep relaxation. It incorporates elements such as setting an intention, body scanning, breath awareness and counting, and visualization (see page 170).

Autonomous sensory meridian response

Autonomous sensory meridian response (ASMR) refers to a tingling sensation along the neck and head that some people feel when exposed to certain stimuli, like a rhythmic whispering voice or patterns of sound. Some colloquially call it a "head orgasm". There have only been a handful of studies on ASMR, including the first study in 2015, which linked the phenomenon to flow state. A 2018 paper describes some overlap between ASMR and mindfulness, but ASMR is not technically meditation. However, a meditation could incorporate elements that elicit the ASMR response. Despite the scant research on it, ASMR is the fifth most-searched term on YouTube worldwide. Hopefully, meditation will catch up as people discover the real-world (and research-backed) benefits.

Join the meditation club

This club is not exclusive, but you may recognize some of its members. From Oprah to the Beatles, countless celebrities, CEOs, pro athletes, and renowned scientists carve out time in their busy lives to meditate after experiencing the benefits.

As the research into meditation grows, its practice is becoming more popular. Of course, meditation has long been mainstream in places like India, where the prime minister has established International Yoga Day on 21 June. Over the past few decades, however, the practice has become popular worldwide and has been infused into many mainstream cultures.

Meditation and mindfulness books regularly remain on bestseller lists for decades, including classic titles such as *The Art of Living* by Vietnamese monk Thích Nhất Hạnh, *The Power of Now* by German author Eckhart Tolle, and *Wherever You Go, There You Are* by American researcher Jon Kabat-Zinn.

Popular novels, too, like those by Japanese author Haruki Murakami, and movies from *The Matrix* to *Star Wars* are often interpreted via the themes of meditation and Buddhist or Hindu philosophy. Indeed, director George Lucas is known to have meditated for over 40 years.

What if I don't have time?

You are not alone. Greek-American author Arianna Huffington writes in an article for website HighExistence, "Finding time for meditation was always a challenge because I was under the impression that I had to 'do' meditation. And I didn't have time for another burdensome thing to 'do'. Fortunately, a friend pointed out one day that we don't 'do' meditation; meditation 'does' us. That opened the door for me."

Likewise, author Elizabeth Gilbert says it took her over 20 years to develop a consistent meditation practice, even after the silent meditation retreat in India she described in her hit book *Eat, Pray, Love*. She was finally able to get into the habit thanks to the convenience of meditation apps, as were many others, including Microsoft co-founder Bill Gates, singer Ricky Martin, and actor Emma Watson. Actor Drew Barrymore tried a different approach; she turned her closet into a meditation room.

Creating a space specifically for meditation in this way can help motivate you to practise, and the results will be worth it. For more tips on how to build consistent practice into your life, see page 28.

What are the real-world benefits?

Although not the goal of meditation, performance enhancement is a common side effect. Tim Ferriss writes in his 2016 book *Tools of Titans* that "more than 80 per cent of the world-class performers I've interviewed have some form of daily meditation or mindfulness habit". And numerous famous examples bear this out.

One of the best basketball players of all time, Michael Jordan, had a mindfulness coach to help him stay focused on the court and in life. Jane Campion, Oscar-winning director of *The Piano*, admits that yoga and meditation have helped her to manage both anxiety and compulsions, while *New York Times* bestselling author Marie Forleo has described how meditation helps her manage her ADHD, saying: "The more time I spend in meditation, the more time I have... It's as though things simplify."

Canadian tennis pro Bianca Andreescu started meditating in her teens. She credits her underdog win against Serena Williams in 2019 to visualization meditation techniques, while Serbian champ Novak Djokovic has said that his meditation routines are "the main points in my day to day... they make me feel good". Meditation comes highly recommended by some of the most successful people on the planet, but you don't need big bucks or a certification to practise. We can all feel its benefits by incorporating it into our daily lives.

The more time I spend in meditation, the more time I have.

How do I get started?

As this book will show, there are many ways you can bring meditation into your daily life. Any time, any place, and for any length of time is a great way to begin! Here are some tips to get you started.

If you are new to meditation, you probably have a lot of questions on how it works and what exactly you are supposed to do. This section will answer more commonly asked questions to help you get started.

What time of day is best?

Many find it is easier to practise meditation in the morning when their mind is fresh, ideally after mindful movement such as yoga or tai chi, to best prepare the body and mind for the day ahead. However, the best time to meditate is the most convenient time for you, so that you will actually do it.

Try fitting in a seated meditation while waiting for your coffee or tea to brew, a lying-down practice during your afternoon break to reset your energy (see page 170), or a quick gratitude-focused meditation before your meal (see page 114). Many find that meditation fits perfectly into a bedtime wind-down routine. Experts say the best way to develop a habit such as meditation is to pair it with an activity you are already doing (see page 28 for more on how this works), so ask yourself, where does meditation fit into your world?

How long should I meditate for?

Some studies suggest that 5–10 minutes a day could make a difference to how you feel. Various traditions advocate practising for an hour or more a day, but for most people it takes years to build up to that. So start small at 5–10 minutes and then build up to 15–20 minutes. Even one-minute meditations throughout your day add up — it all counts!

What position should I be in?

The common image of meditation is sitting in a traditional cross-legged position on the ground (see opposite), but that isn't comfortable for many people. The best position for you to meditate in is whichever you find most comfortable and relaxing, and whichever is most convenient for you. There are numerous variations on seated meditations you can try, such as kneeling on the ground, sitting on a cushion, or in a chair, as well as options that don't involve sitting at all. Try them all and discover which is best for you.

Easy pose (Sukhasana)

Easy pose, or sukhasana, is what most people imagine when they think of meditation. It involves sitting on the ground with the legs crossed and the spine tall. This is not easy for many people today, especially if they sit at a computer for most of the day, but there are options to make it more accessible, like using pillows under your hips, or leaning against a wall.

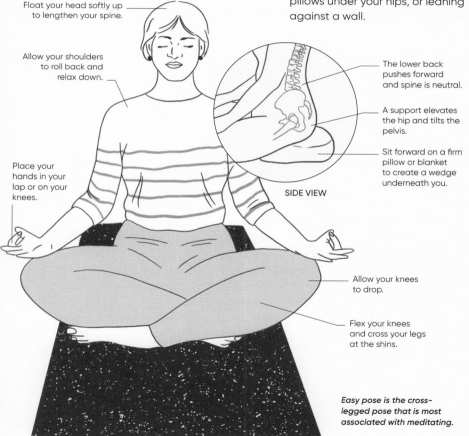

Float your head softly up to lengthen your spine.

Allow your shoulders to roll back and relax down.

Place your hands in your lap or on your knees.

The lower back pushes forward and spine is neutral.

A support elevates the hip and tilts the pelvis.

Sit forward on a firm pillow or blanket to create a wedge underneath you.

SIDE VIEW

Allow your knees to drop.

Flex your knees and cross your legs at the shins.

Easy pose is the cross-legged pose that is most associated with meditating.

Thunderbolt Pose (Vajrasana)

Another traditional meditation posture is vajrasana, also called the "thunderbolt pose" due to the shape the body makes in this kneeling position. Vajrasana can be adapted by sitting on a yoga block or by putting a rolled blanket or bolster lengthways between your shins and knees to help alleviate the pressure on the joints.

Sit tall and align your ears over your shoulders by allowing your head to float up.

Draw your shoulders back and lift your chest up and forward.

Rest your hands on your thighs and gaze forwards.

Try putting something under your buttocks if you feel pressure in your joints.

Kneel on the floor, sitting on your feet or with your feet either side of your hips.

Thunderbolt pose relieves pressure from the knees and gets its name from the shape your body creates when kneeling.

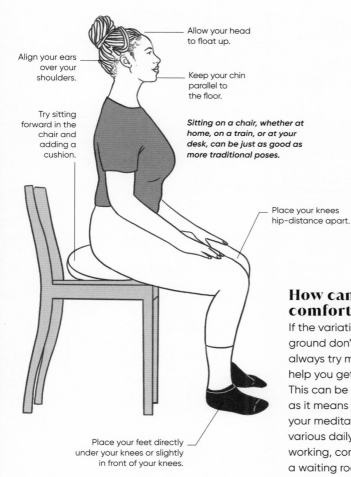

Allow your head to float up.

Align your ears over your shoulders.

Keep your chin parallel to the floor.

Try sitting forward in the chair and adding a cushion.

Sitting on a chair, whether at home, on a train, or at your desk, can be just as good as more traditional poses.

Place your knees hip-distance apart.

Place your feet directly under your knees or slightly in front of your knees.

How can I get more comfortable?

If the variations of sitting on the ground don't work for you, you can always try meditating in a chair to help you get more comfortable. This can be a very convenient pose, as it means you can combine your meditation practice with various daily activities, such as working, commuting, or sitting in a waiting room.

Everyday Chair Meditation

The way we sit in a chair while meditating is different to how we sit at the computer. This method gives you an opportunity to sit tall and counter the rounding-forward position that often occurs when we are typing an email.

Can't leave the office? Try meditating in your office chair between meetings.

What do I do with my hands?

You can often place your hands in your lap, in whatever position is comfortable. Palms up can invite a sense of openness into your practice, perhaps helping you feel more energized. Palms down can set the intention of feeling grounded and calming your energy down.

Hand placement in specific gestures is called mudra. In yoga, mudras are gestures of the hands or body that seal in energy. Traditionally, they set specific intentions like peace, relaxation, or focus. Bhairava mudra, for example – laying the right-hand palm inside the left – is intended to cultivate a sense of unity. (Explore a meditation practice with mudras on page 77.) Mudras are also said to have healing powers, such as lowering blood pressure. Although research has not confirmed this, it is feasible that by setting an intention and shifting your focus to something, it makes it more likely to happen.

Where do I look?

A drishti is a point of focus for your gaze. With the eyes open, you might gaze at a spot on the ground a few metres away or at an object like a candle or mountain ahead of you to stay present (see page 140 for more on visual focal points during meditation). Alternatively, you could look up towards your third eye to encourage focus and invite intuition (see page 66). When sitting in your office, you could focus on a tree outside your window.

How do I develop a consistent practice?

You might expect the conventional advice for developing a consistent meditation habit to be to choose a specific time to meditate or set a goal of how long you will practice daily. If that works for you, great, but evidence suggests there are more efficient and effective methods.

James Clear, bestselling author of *Atomic Habits*, suggests focusing on who you want to become with your new habit. By practising meditation, you become what you cultivate: more present, focused, compassionate, and peaceful.

MYTH BUSTER
You have to close your eyes

Closing your eyes can help bring your awareness inwards by blocking out your sense of sight. However, if this is uncomfortable, you can always keep your eyes open (or partially open) with a soft gaze. With the eyes open, you can focus your gaze to different drishtis, as described left.

As you realize the transformative benefits of meditation, you will probably aspire to fit a more formal daily practice into your routine. Start small, with just a few minutes, and build up over time, or try the habit pairing technique below.

Habit pairing

Do you ever skip brushing your teeth? It's probably rare, since that is a deeply ingrained habit. And you can use that to your advantage. Research suggests that piggybacking a new activity with a habit you already have helps new habits stick. Eventually, you will look at meditation as something as routine as brushing your teeth. You may begin to associate the two together as one event: wake up, brush teeth, meditate... brush teeth, meditate, go to bed. (You can even be mindful while brushing; see page 134.) To pair an existing habit with your meditation practice, try this:

1. Set your intention: You can simply say this in your head, or write it down and put it somewhere you can see it – perhaps in the kitchen or bathroom. Complete the sentence: *"Before/after/while I [____] I will meditate."* For example:
"Before my first coffee, I will meditate."
"After I write my to-do list for the day, I will meditate."

"While I watch the sunset, I will meditate."

2. Once you have decided which habit to pair with your practice, choose a simple meditation from the book. Breathwork such as elongated exhales (see page 51) is a good place to start, or focus on visuals (see page 140) or sounds (see page 137). Overcome barriers to practice by making it easier – for example, keep this book on your nightstand, put meditation apps on your phone's homepage, or find an accountability partner to help you.

3. If you get out of the habit, reassess. Is this the best pairing for you or do you need to try something new? Pause, reflect, and refine. And remember, it takes time.

How long does it take to build a habit?

You may have heard that it takes 21, 30, or 66 days to build a habit, but author James Clear says: "The honest answer is: forever. Because once you stop doing it, it is no longer a habit. A habit is a lifestyle to be lived, not a finish line to be crossed." Consider meditation a journey of lifelong learning that doesn't change who you are, but allows your highest self to emerge.

Is there special breathing?

Generally, you want to breathe comfortably and with ease during meditation. There are numerous ways to optimize your breath, and strategic breathing practices to prepare your body and mind for meditation.

Typically, you will breathe through your nose while meditating, unless instructed otherwise for a specific technique. However, if you are congested or unable to nose breathe, mouth breathing is a temporary back-up.

Low and slow breathing

Your ideal breath meets your metabolic needs for whatever you are doing, which means it is faster when you're running up the stairs than it is while you're at rest in a seated meditation. Generally, for meditation, we want to breathe low and slow. Breathe low by allowing your abdomen to move with your breath, commonly called diaphragmatic breathing or belly breathing. This is our natural way of breathing, allowing your ribs and abdomen to move three-dimensionally. As we get older, society tells us to suck in our stomachs and we lose this natural, healthy movement of the diaphragm, but we can re-learn how to breathe in this way through awareness and practice.

Breathe slow to encourage relaxation and clear thinking. During meditation (and throughout your day as you remember), you could try to consciously slow your breathing rate as much as is comfortable.

The benefits of breathing through your nose

- **It filters the air,** *trapping pollutants and microscopic invaders with hairs and mucus.*
- **It warms and humidifies the air,** *making it more comfortable to breathe.*
- **It reduces dry mouth,** *compared to mouth breathing.*
- **It increases our intake of nitric oxide,** *a molecule released naturally in our nasal and sinus pathways that acts as a vasodilator, leading to enhanced relaxation, circulation, oxygen transportation, and immune function.*
- **It improves focus** *and concentration during tasks.*

Intentional breathing

Breathwork is a term often used in the West for intentional breathing practices, which are done to optimize the breath or achieve a desired result (such as relaxation or increased energy). Pranayama is a yogic breathing system that is often used to prepare properly for meditation, as outlined in the eight limbs of yoga (see page 168).

Many of these dedicated breathing practices are included in this book, and each one can help you with a specific issue. They include:
Elongated exhales for calming your nervous system (see page 51).

Alternate nostril breathing to improve concentration (see page 68).
Triangle breathing and **single nostril breathing** to fight fatigue (see page 75).
Box breathing for high-pressure situations (see page 86).
Bee breath (bhramari) to lower blood pressure (see page 113).
Cooling breath (sitali or sitkari) for hot flushes (see page 122).
Physiological sigh to release anxiety or stress (see page 135).

The benefits of low and slow breathing

- *Improves blood circulation.*
- *Improves lymph circulation, which can aid immunity.*
- *Lowers blood pressure.*
- *Slows heart rate.*
- *Improves heart-rate variability, promoting cardiac resilience.*
- *Improves ventilation efficiency.*
- *Improves focus and learning.*

EXHALE

INHALE

On the inhale, the ribcage expands.

The diaphragm engages downwards.

The abdomen expands.

Diaphragmatic breathing

Is meditation the secret to ageing well?

Research on the ageing process has skyrocketed in the past decade. As we live longer, we want to live better, and the science suggests that meditation can help us do that.

Scientists believe that if they can better understand ageing, they can address many age-related diseases, which would not only improve our lives, but also help relieve pressure on our healthcare services. Some of this research has looked at the long-term effects of meditation and seems to indicate that it can slow, and sometimes even reverse, aspects of the ageing process. Of course, ageing is a privilege, and no approach should be considered "anti-ageing", but rather "pro-ageing" – a way to help us age gracefully and healthfully.

Can meditation help my brain as I get older?

Many areas of your brain tend to shrink and degrade with age. However, Harvard neuroscientist Dr Sara Lazar and others compared MRI brain scans to show that multiple areas of the brain have slower ageing in meditators compared to people who don't meditate. This suggests that meditation may slow or even prevent some of the natural degradation of brain tissue that occurs with age.

While it is likely that other factors are also involved, such as lifestyle and diet (and it's worth noting that meditation also seems to encourage a healthy lifestyle), a growing body of research suggests that meditation and the associated mindset could significantly contribute to slowing brain ageing.

Older meditators seem to have slower brain ageing than non-meditators.

Promoting neuroplasticity

Your brain's ability to adapt is thanks to the fact that it is malleable – or "plastic", as it is often described. A key mechanism through which meditation protects the ageing brain is its ability to promote this "neuroplasticity". Meditation leads to physical adaptations in the nervous tissue in your brain by changing or creating new connections between nerve cells. Just as exercise builds your muscle tissue, meditation builds the density of your brain tissue. Doing and learning new things – such as joining a yoga class, learning a new language, or juggling – also encourages neuroplasticity. Meditation is an effective promoter of neuroplasticity, and what is particularly remarkable is where in the brain it brings about these changes. Through meditation, neural connectivity builds in precisely the same brain areas that tend to degrade with age and malfunction with stress, depression, anxiety, and chronic pain. Meditation rebuilds neural connections in the memory centre (the hippocampus) and areas associated with cognition and focus, such as the prefrontal cortex. In other words, meditation literally changes your brain.

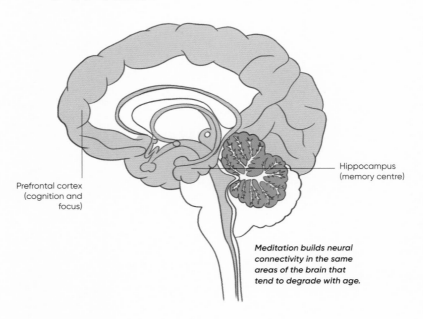

Prefrontal cortex
(cognition and
focus)

Hippocampus
(memory centre)

*Meditation builds neural
connectivity in the same
areas of the brain that
tend to degrade with age.*

Improving memory

Another extraordinary effect that meditation can have on the brain is to improve our memory, especially as we get older. Meditation has been shown to enhance memory in healthy adults, and increase the volume of the hippocampus and its memory capacity through neuroplasticity. Meditation also strengthens attention and cognitive reasoning in older adults.

Dementia and meditation

Promising research shows that meditation could help delay the onset and slow the progression of dementia and general cognitive decline, while improving quality of life. In particular, preliminary evidence suggests that meditation could help in the earliest stages of dementia. See page 76 for more on the research and a practice for memory care.

Just as exercise builds muscle tissue, meditation builds the density of your brain tissue.

MYTH BUSTER
I'm too old to meditate

It's never too late to learn to meditate. Research shows older adults can see measurable results from taking up the practice. One study published in Nature in 2021 introduced participants aged over 65 to a mindfulness-based stress-reduction (MBSR) programme. Researchers took blood samples before and after, and with just four weeks of MBSR practice, participants had positive changes in cognition-related gene activity. People of all ages can enjoy benefits from starting a meditation practice.

Can meditation help me stay younger?

We cannot change our chronological age – the number of years we have lived – but we can influence our biological age. Our biological age combines our genetics (the genes we're born with) and our epigenetics (how behaviours and environment affect our genes). Meditation has been shown to have a beneficial effect on both of them.

Nature and nurture

Your genes are not your destiny. Both nature and nurture play a role, and scientists predict that nurture (your lifestyle) seems to play a more significant role than previously thought. According to identical-twin studies, scientists predict that genes contribute only 7–25 per cent to longevity. Your lifestyle and mindset seem to be the most important factors by far. And practising meditation and mindfulness tends to encourage healthy lifestyle choices.

Epigenetics refers to how behaviours and environment can affect how your genes work, including which genes are expressed or activated. Meditation has been shown to affect you on a genetic level, discouraging unhealthy gene expression (like chronic diseases) and encouraging healthier genes to be expressed (like those related to good immune function). One study measured the biological ages of meditators and non-meditators by taking blood samples. The researchers found that long-term meditators had lower biological ages, suggesting that practising meditation long-term could be a "preventative strategy for age-related chronic disease".

Telomere length

Meditation seems to keep your cells acting younger, too. Research shows that telomeres (the caps that protect chromosomes' ends) usually shorten with age (as well as increased stress). When cells divide over the years, telomeres tend to get shorter. So as we age, we have more chromosomes with short telomeres. Eventually, when telomeres become critically short, it can lead to cell death (called apoptosis), or the cell can become senescent – these are called zombie cells, which aren't dead or alive; they just wreak havoc on nearby cells.

Researcher Elissa Epel, PhD, and her team at the University of California, San Francisco, have concluded that mindfulness meditation can help keep telomeres longer. The reduced cognitive stress and increased positive states of mind meditation induces seem to promote telomere maintenance by increasing the activity of the enzyme called telomerase, which can delay or reverse cellular ageing.

Longer healthspan

Overall, meditation encourages healthy ageing and may help you live longer (increasing your lifespan). But, more importantly, practising meditation can help increase your healthspan. Your healthspan is the number of years you live in good health, thriving and being able to do the activities you love.

Meditation may help increase your "healthspan": the number of years you live in good health.

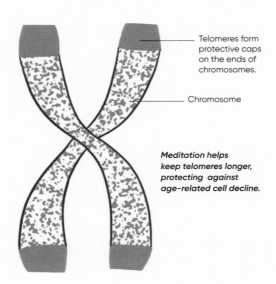

Telomeres form protective caps on the ends of chromosomes.

Chromosome

Meditation helps keep telomeres longer, protecting against age-related cell decline.

Your brain when meditating

When you are sitting still and meditating, it may seem like nothing much is going on inside your head, but your brain is in fact quite active, with electrical activity taking place and measurable shifts in its neurochemistry.

Some of the most compelling research on meditation looks at how it can change your brain in many ways – with both short-term *brain state* changes (after mere minutes of practice) and long-term *brain trait* changes (usually after months or years of consistent practice). The hectic modern world can lead to a busy mind filled with distractions and worries, but meditation can shift your brain state towards calm amid this chaos, leading to long-term wellbeing.

What happens to my brain while I'm meditating?

As soon as you begin meditating, your brain state alters. Electrical changes occur as certain brain areas and circuits are activated. Within minutes (and continuing for hours and even days afterwards) chemical shifts occur – including reduced cortisol levels – resulting in more balanced biochemistry.

Electrical changes

You are an energetic being with electrical energy cascading through your body and brain via conductive nerve cells. The activity of these electrical currents creates and reinforces neural pathways. Over time, pathways in your brain can become stuck and maladaptive pathways can develop, such as when we can't stop ruminating. Practising meditation helps to break such maladaptive paths and promote healthy ones, often leading to positive lifestyle choices. It is important to note that different patterns of activity and chemical changes have been documented with varying styles of meditation, and only certain types of brain changes have been evaluated to date, so there is still a lot left to explore.

Brain regions and networks

Initially, neuroscientists focused on how meditation impacts specific brain regions and their functions. However, brain activity of any kind isn't isolated to certain areas, but rather works in intricate networks of interconnected regions. In the past decade, cutting-edge neuroscience has revealed that meditation can induce significant changes in these networks. It tends to deactivate and dampen connectivity between areas related to mind-wandering, rumination, and self-referential processing or "me" thinking (known as the **default mode network**). When the mind inevitably does meander, the network in charge of determining the importance of the sensory information (the **salience network**) alerts the meditator, prompting them to disengage from spontaneous thought and return to the meditation focus. The network involved in controlling attention (the **central executive network**) takes over when the meditator maintains sustained focus on one thing, such as the breath, a visual, or a mantra. The process repeats when the mind gets distracted again.

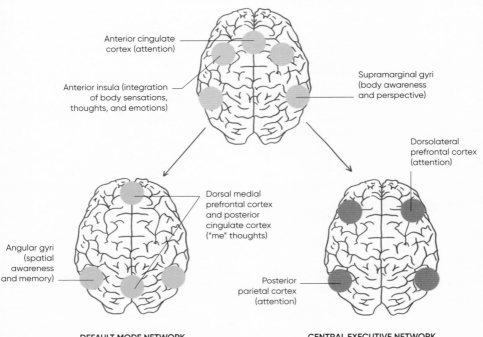

SALIENCE NETWORK
Determines if something is important and facilitates switching between networks.

Anterior cingulate cortex (attention)

Anterior insula (integration of body sensations, thoughts, and emotions)

Supramarginal gyri (body awareness and perspective)

Dorsolateral prefrontal cortex (attention)

Dorsal medial prefrontal cortex and posterior cingulate cortex ("me" thoughts)

Angular gyri (spatial awareness and memory)

Posterior parietal cortex (attention)

DEFAULT MODE NETWORK
Involved in mind-wandering and self-focused thinking. Tends to be deactivated by meditation.

CENTRAL EXECUTIVE NETWORK
Involved in controlling attention. Tends to be activated by meditation.

Brainwaves

Scientists use tools like an electroencephalogram (EEG) to measure brainwave activity in real time. Basically, researchers hook electrodes to the heads of meditators to measure oscillations of electricity in various areas of the brain. Although different meditation styles have varying patterns of activity, overall, many styles of meditation are associated with the increased dominance of alpha- and theta-wave frequencies, which can help enhance relaxation, learning, and mental wellbeing.

FREQUENCY	CHARACTERISTICS	RELEVANCE IN MEDITATION
Gamma (35+ Hz)	Peak focus and memory consolidation	Particularly seen in compassion meditation and especially in long-term practitioners.
Beta (12–35 Hz)	Alert and concentrating, as in a goal-oriented task or in conversation	Typically, meditation moves your brain out of these frequencies in most areas of the brain.
Alpha (8–12 Hz)	Relaxed	Meditation often brings us into the alpha waves initially and can lead to the dominance of alpha waves after practice.
Theta (4–8 Hz)	Creative problem-solving	Meditation, particularly in more advanced practitioners, can cause theta-wave dominance, especially in areas responsible for monitoring internal experiences.
Delta (less than 4 Hz)	Deep, dreamless sleep	Although delta waves are less present during meditation, they have been shown to be present in yoga nidra (see page 170), which guides you into a waking sleep-like state. Also, meditation has been shown to improve sleep quality, which means you might notice deeper sleep.

Chemical changes

Meditation changes your brain chemistry, influencing your body's biochemistry. It measurably impacts your neurotransmitters, which are present between nerve cells to help them communicate, as well as hormones that circulate in the bloodstream and have widespread effects throughout the body. Here are some of the biochemical changes meditation tends to cause:

Stress hormones decrease: Meditation reduces adrenaline and cortisol. Adrenaline is a stress hormone that puts you in overdrive to face emergencies (real and imagined). Our cortisol levels fluctuate naturally throughout the day, but chronically high levels of cortisol are associated with long-term stress, inflammation, fatigue, irritability, and holding on to excess fat.

GABA increases: Gamma-aminobutyric acid (GABA) is an inhibitory neurotransmitter. Increased GABA counteracts anxiety and stress, leading to more relaxation.

BDNF increases: Brain-derived neurotrophic factor (BDNF) is a protein that helps neurotransmitters do their job. Increased BDNF levels can lead to new neuron connections and growth.

Serotonin increases: Serotonin is associated with happiness and positive mood. One study has suggested that regular meditation practitioners have higher serotonin levels compared to the baseline in control groups and even higher levels after meditation practice.

Endorphins increase: From the words "endogenous", meaning "from within", and morphine (a strong analgesic), these "feel-good" chemicals enhance our sense of wellbeing.

Oxytocin increases: Sometimes called the love or cuddle hormone, oxytocin helps us to feel connected and bonded with others. It is also anti-inflammatory, antioxidant, and good for the immune system. Compassion meditation tends to increase oxytocin levels.

Dopamine is regulated, and often increases: This acts as your reward system and it is particularly released in anticipation of pleasure. Dopamine dysfunction is associated with addiction, depression, and anxiety. Meditation has been shown to modulate brain areas that produce and respond to dopamine.

Multiple
prefrontal
regions
(emotional
regulation)

Striatum
(emotional
regulation and
attention
control)

Posterior
cingulate cortex
(self-awareness)

Anterior
cingulate
cortex
(attention
control)

The brain benefits of consistent meditation

With frequent and consistent meditation, short-term changes lead to long-term results, or what neuroscientists call brain trait changes. Some adaptations in the brain have been documented after just a few weeks of meditation; others can take months or years to appear.

Beyond the electrical and chemical changes, there are also measurable *physical* brain changes from regular practice. There is a saying among neuroscientists: "Neurons that fire together, wire together." The neural activity that happens in real-time when you meditate adds up. Where attention goes, energy literally goes

The highlighted regions of the brain are strengthened by meditation, enhancing focus, memory, and the regulation of emotions, stress, and pain.

(in the form of electrical activity) and connections in those areas grow stronger. You are rewiring neural circuits to strengthen connections, which ultimately builds brain tissue density in critical areas, as seen in MRI imagery. These structural changes represent such real-world benefits as enhanced focus, cognition, and memory, as well as the ability to better manage stress, pain, and emotions – especially when life gets tough.

Where attention goes, energy literally goes, and connections in those areas grow stronger.

INNER LABORATORY
Track your brainwaves

You don't have to be in the lab to get real-time neurofeedback; you can experiment at home with simple EEG devices, such as the Muse brain-sensing headband. It lets you know when you have relaxed brainwaves and helps you recognize when your mind wanders and get back on track. You can create a home laboratory with Muse, a blood-pressure cuff (see page 112), your smart watch for sleep data (see page 103), or just your own fingers to check your pulse.

Change your mind (and your life)

Your brain accounts for just 2 per cent of your body weight, but remarkably it takes 20 per cent of your energy to function. When your mind is overactive or overstimulated, meditation can provide a brain break.

Meditation not only changes your brain physically and chemically; it also changes the way you think and interact with the world. Through meditation, you can delve into key philosophical and metaphysical perspectives and explore its positive, life-transforming effects.

Meditation can help with self-reflection

Learning meditation can help you develop self-awareness, enhancing your ability to:
- think about your thinking.
- be aware that you are aware.
- be aware of your thinking patterns and processes.

Meditation also teaches you how to observe the internal dialogue in your head – and not automatically believe it, which is a helpful skill for improving mental health. You learn that you are not defined by your thoughts. In other words, meditation gets you out of your head.

This deep self-awareness optimizes how you think and learn. As you practise different meditations in this book or with a teacher, you will gain insights into your own thought tendencies, habits, and personal obstacles to staying present and feeling at peace.

Does meditation get rid of the ego?

One of the claimed benefits of meditation is that it dissolves your ego. Studies reveal that it reduces (though does not completely eliminate) activity in the "me" centres of the brain, particularly for experienced meditators. Thoughts of *my* opinions, *my* stuff, *my* relationships, *my* likes on social media, and other self-centred mind chatter, start to quieten. Attractions and aversions have a looser grip on you, resulting in less extreme ups and downs. Meditation can also help you take things less personally and feel a sense of equanimity – even amid life's challenges.

What if I experience difficult emotions?

Sitting still and looking inwards can be uncomfortable. Tendencies to overwork, overthink, and get stuck in overdrive can be coping mechanisms to avoid painful thoughts. If challenging emotions come up when you start meditating, seek a qualified meditation teacher and talk to a good therapist.

If you have a history of severe trauma, psychosis, bipolar disorder, or schizophrenia, consult your medical team, get counselling, and seek a well-trained meditation teacher before you start. Meditation can help you, as it teaches vital regulation skills, but start slowly under supervision, and gradually increase the intensity as tolerated.

Is mind-wandering bad?

Mind-wandering is when you are thinking about something other than the present moment. This skill could be considered an evolutionary advantage, as it allows us to reflect on the past, plan for future goals, and be creative. Chatting through a situation in your head can help you come to a logical solution and daydreaming can be a relaxing escape. The problem comes when you can't turn it off. When that little voice in your head follows you uninvited into the shower, work, or moments with your partner, it gets distracting and draining. This imaginary "friend" can talk way too much, often in annoying loops.

Research suggests that about 47 per cent of our waking hours are spent mind-wandering, and one groundbreaking study found that this mental time-travelling tended to be the cause of unhappiness. The study, entitled "A wandering mind is an unhappy mind", published in the top-tier journal *Science*, concluded, "The ability to think about what is not happening is a cognitive achievement that comes at an emotional cost."

Nearly half of our waking hours are spent mind-wandering.

Other research, meanwhile, has found that mind-wandering, especially to negative thoughts, is associated with accelerated ageing and an increased risk of mental health conditions. Meditation is a clear antidote as it teaches the skill of redirecting our attention to the present moment. Being mindful and in flow in your everyday activities – even seemingly mundane ones – is the opposite of distraction. The philosophy of meditation teaches us that true happiness is found in living

Focused attention: Maintaining focus on object of attention.

Spontaneous thought: Mind-wandering.

Reorientation of awareness: Refocusing attention back to the present.

The cycle of focused attention

About 47% of our waking hours are spent mind-wandering. Meditation can help redirect our attention back to the present.

Awareness of ongoing thought: Becoming aware of mind-wandering.

in the present moment. Research also suggests that cultivating compassion through meditation can reduce mind-wandering and may help our thoughts and actions be less self-centred and more caring.

How could meditation change my life?

Ultimately, meditation helps us tap into an inner strength to face life's stresses, helping us to emerge stronger and wiser. It also heightens our awareness, including that of our internal state, leading to healthier lifestyle choices. Amid an epidemic of lifestyle-related diseases, such as diabetes, heart disease, and various mental health conditions, the positive behaviour changes from meditation and mindfulness can help manage and even prevent them before they start. As you make better choices on a small scale, meditation can become a catalyst for other big changes in your life. Of course, no one and nothing external will give you true happiness and fulfilment. They are within. Once our basic needs are met, there is no sense in pinning your hopes of happiness on the idea of perfect circumstances or a utopia; instead, we have the option to cultivate eudaimonia – the ancient Greek concept of living well and flourishing. Meditation promotes eudaimonic happiness, which is not fleeting or dependent on outside things, but instead fosters optimal psychological functioning, resilience, and personal growth. Fitting in meditation and mindfulness can help you solve practical daily problems, as you will see in this book, but practice ultimately leads you on a transformative journey towards deeper meaning, purpose, and inner peace.

Meditation helps us tap into an inner strength to face life's stresses.

CHAPTER 2

MEDITATION FOR A HEALTHY MIND

Now, let's move beyond theory and into practices to support a healthy mind. In a fast-paced, demanding world, meditation teaches the skill of sitting with difficult emotions, rather than distracting yourself from them.

Ultimately, emotions are teachers. Stress teaches us how strong we are, anger helps us set healthy boundaries, anxiety asks us to be present with what is rather than what might be, and envy illuminates who we aspire to become. In this chapter, you'll find practices to support you through each of these emotions and many real-world scenarios – including mourning a loss, being ghosted, prepping for an exam, and overcoming stage fright.

Repetition rewires your brain, and practice makes progress (not perfect). When it comes to meditation, practice also makes you present. So now, experience meditations to help you navigate life challenges and give you brain power when you need it most.

Ease stress and find calm

Feeling impatient? Dealing with difficult people? Plane about to take off? Unfortunately, we can't control everything that happens to us (and we definitely can't control other people), but we can control our breath and how our nervous system responds to stressful situations.

When we feel overwhelmed, our sympathetic nervous system can be triggered, causing symptoms such as a racing heart, higher blood pressure, and fast breathing, known as the "fight or flight" response. This can be disruptive and distressing, especially if it happens often or seems disproportionate to the situation. Meditation can help ease this response through extended exhales and a safe environment. This helps to cultivate a calm state by influencing the vagus nerve – the cranial nerve that regulates many vital organs and is involved in the relaxing effect of the nervous system's parasympathetic response, also called "rest and digest" mode.

Influencing your vagus nerve

Even a quick breathing exercise can counteract overwhelming feelings. Each breath you take sets a rhythm for your body systems to respond to, like a dynamic dance. Changing the rhythm, like doubling your exhales, changes how electrical currents move through your nervous system, affecting your heart, gut, mood, energy levels, and more.

Inhale: Sympathetic

With each and every inhale you take, blood is shunted to your heart and lungs to help them function. Pressure receptors called baroreceptors sense that increase in pressure and respond by signalling to increase your sympathetic nervous system activity to handle the stress.

Exhale: Parasympathetic

With each exhale, the vagus nerve influences your heart, slowing your heartrate. This essentially presses a metaphorical brake pedal, putting you more into the parasympathetic response to help you conserve energy. There is a slight relaxation in the body with each exhale, which explains why elongating your exhales is so calming (see opposite).

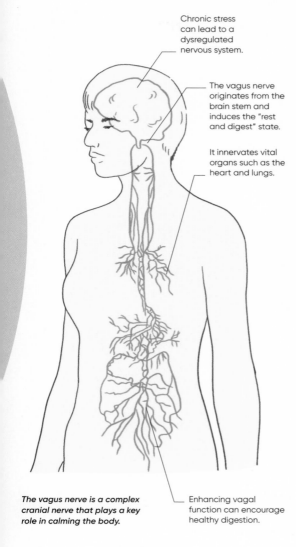

Chronic stress can lead to a dysregulated nervous system.

The vagus nerve originates from the brain stem and induces the "rest and digest" state.

It innervates vital organs such as the heart and lungs.

The vagus nerve is a complex cranial nerve that plays a key role in calming the body.

Enhancing vagal function can encourage healthy digestion.

A QUICK DE-STRESS

In about a minute (or even less!) you can experience profound physiological benefits when you're feeling stressed. Try it out while you read.

1. Elongate your spine. You can be seated or standing – it doesn't matter. Just be tall but not stiff.

2. Notice your natural breath for a moment. Is the inhale or exhale longer? Or are they about the same length? Just notice.

3. Elongate the length of your exhale. Try for twice as long as your inhale, but it doesn't have to be exact – as long as the exhale is longer than the inhale, you are doing great. Experiment for a moment to find a length that doesn't feel forced. Start by inhaling for two counts, and exhaling for four. If that is comfortable, try inhaling for three counts and exhaling for six. If that feels comfortable, increase to four counts on the inhale, and eight counts on the exhale.

4. Keep experimenting and choose the ratio that feels right for you today. If you are a singer or have ever played a wind instrument, you might be able to take even longer breaths. Counting is optional.

Feeling anger and frustration

Anger is a powerful and natural emotion. It is an adaptive response to a threat, causing stress hormones like adrenaline to generate heated energy and provoke you to take action if necessary. Sometimes, however, we need to rein it in.

Anger becomes a problem when your mind perpetuates frustration, turning it into rage. Before you know it, you are thinking about all the reasons you are justified in your anger – or worse, you could act from anger and hurt others. Mental loops fuel anger and its negative effects on your wellbeing. So instead of continuing that argument in your head, use mindfulness to stop thoughts in their tracks and practise meditation to build the skill of rapid emotional regulation.

Don't drink poison

You may know the old saying that holding on to your anger is like drinking poison and expecting the other person to die. A short burst of anger can be useful to motivate action, but prolonged anger constricts blood vessels, leading to chronic high blood pressure and inflammation and causing your heart to pound rapidly, which damages your body. You may feel righteous in your rage (you may even be justified), but isn't drinking the poison counterproductive in the long-term?

Breaking past blame

If you catch yourself playing the blame game, dwelling on the reasons the other person is wrong or has wronged you, the common advice is to let go and forgive. That's easier said than done, of course. It takes inner work to move from blame to forgiveness. But if persistent anger is like drinking poison, forgiveness is the medicine you need to heal.

Cultivate compassion

Finding compassion can help you feel better. It may help to remember that hurt people hurt people. You may be thinking, "That doesn't mean it is OK." But cultivating compassion for them doesn't mean becoming complacent to injustices or avoiding action. It may lead to letting go and realizing that inaction is the best path, but empathy can also take the edge off your anger so you can move forward with calm, appropriate action. Practise compassion with a loving-kindness meditation (see page 79).

FEEL IT

The first step is learning to recognize and feel anger arising. Practise now so you can mindfully notice your personal warning signs in the heat of the moment.

1. Notice how your body feels when you are angry or remembering a situation that makes you angry.
• How is your heart rate affected?
• How about your breath?
• How do you feel overall?

2. Do a body scan from head to toe and notice where you feel it most in your body. Your head? Throat? Chest? Abdomen? Hips?

3. What do you feel, beyond simply anger? Physically, it might feel warm, tight, bubbling... Emotionally, there may be other feelings, such as sadness or disappointment.

4. Feel the full complexity of the anger. Begin to slow your breath and relax into whatever is present.

Use mindfulness to stop thoughts in their tracks.

FINDING FORGIVENESS

Here is an 8–10-minute process to move from anger to acceptance to forgiveness and beyond.

1. Sit comfortably and set a timer for two minutes.

2. Consider the person you are angry with (this may even be yourself). Immediately, the thoughts will probably spin. Be with the feelings of judgement, disapproval, blame, fault, or whatever you feel right now. Notice and feel them (both emotionally and physically).

3. Reset the timer for another two minutes, then slow your breath and invite a sense of acceptance. This is not accepting that what happened was right or OK but simply that it did happen as a matter of fact.

4. Reset the timer. Now, challenge yourself to consider the ways you appreciate that person and/or the lessons they have taught you. Thoughts of blame will likely creep in but come back to being open to any wisdom that may arise. Perhaps it is a better sense of boundaries, acceptance, or patience.

5. Reset the timer, then come back to inviting a sense of acceptance – of your breath, sounds, sensations, and whatever arises as you rest in open awareness.

6. Consider writing your lessons down or talking it through with a trusted confidant.

Depression and feeling down

When darkness takes over, it can be hard to imagine that light exists. Meditation can help during difficult times, such as when we mourn a loss, can't stop fixating on something that happened, or feel down and don't know why.

When you're feeling low you may long for a quick fix that can snap you out of this feeling right away, but evidence suggests that practising meditation can help over time. Specific techniques such as visualization and mindfulness of body sensations can interrupt rumination, and affirmations can rewrite the narrative in our minds. Research indicates that meditation can also complement your regular medical and therapeutic care. Don't be afraid to seek professional help, as clinical depression is a serious (and very common) condition. You are not alone with these struggles, even though it may feel that way at times. There is hope.

At one with nature

Our internal experience mirrors nature, as we are part of the natural world. Indeed, the winter months are known to contribute to seasonal depression. However, the weather, the seasons, and our inner states are all ever-changing.

VISUALIZE THE SKY

Try this brief visualization to reflect on the true nature of things.

1. Sit tall and observe your inner state now. Notice your current feelings (both emotional and physical). Sometimes, like a child needing attention, feelings need acknowledgement. Feel whatever is present for several deep breaths.

2. Imagine looking up at the sky. When you are feeling dark and stormy, it is like there are ominous clouds looming.

3. Visualize above the clouds a serene and radiant blue sky. Recognize that the blue sky and shining sun are always there, even when you can't see them. Notice how it feels in your body to rest in the vision of a vast, blue sky for at least a minute.

Life-affirming mantras

Affirmations can be used as mantras throughout your day to help shift perspective. Mantra meditation involves repetition of a word, sound, or phrase. In the yoga tradition, a mantra is often said in Sanskrit due to the inherent resonance of the language. For example, "So Hum" signifies a sense of union with the universe. However, even simply repeating the word "one" has been shown to have powerful effects. You can choose any word or phrase you want. You may find it particularly helpful to select a positive affirmation that helps you see things in a new light.

SWITCH THE SCRIPT

Repeat your chosen mantra word or phrase silently or audibly throughout the day as and when you need it, or use it during a formal mantra meditation by repeating for 5–10 minutes.

"This too shall pass."

"Thoughts are not facts."

"I am not my thoughts."

"Right now, I am OK."

"What if it all works out?"

"I am not alone."

"I am one with the universe."

"I can and I will heal."

"One."

"So Hum."

"Love."

"Peace."

ONE-MINUTE MEDITATION
Illuminating loneliness

Whenever you feel lonely, visualize a small light within you. Notice where your mind chooses for it to originate and what colour it shines. With each inhale, feel it burning more brightly; with each exhale it shines first throughout your body, then beyond your body to fill the room, the building, the city, and beyond, touching the lights of others. Then, envision a spaceship's view of Earth, looking down at the luminous light as it expands with each breath. Then, simply rest and bask in the warmth.

Getting through grief

Grieving is the natural process after any significant loss, including the death of a loved one. As proposed by psychiatrist Elisabeth Kübler-Ross in her book *On Death and Dying* in 1969, there are five key stages of grief: denial, anger, bargaining, depression, and acceptance. Technically, however, there are more than five stages, often including an initial shock, and post-acceptance reintegration, hope, and a renewed life purpose. In the real world, grief doesn't follow a perfect model or linear path but instead can feel like a spiral or wave of emotions that includes depression. Sometimes the only way out is through; use the following meditation to go through the process of grief.

Affirmations can rewrite the narrative in our minds.

HONOUR YOUR GRIEF

Whatever stage of grief you are in, rather than push it down, sit with it and allow any wisdom to emerge.

1. Sit tall and notice any physical sensations in your body.

2. Let go of any facade or facial expression you hold throughout the day. Allow your jaw to drop, your eyes to sink back, and feel the worry lines on your forehead release. Imagine the skin and muscles are draping over your skull. When you physically let go of the mask you wear for the world, your true emotions may surface.

3. Be with what is for several minutes. No need to hold back tears or to feel you "should be" crying or feeling anything in particular. Notice which stage(s) of grief you are in.

4. Let the wisdom of your breath take over and do what it needs.

5. Let the grief do its work and just observe what comes up for several minutes.

6. To end, bow your head down and rest the contents of your skull in the tender space of your heart in honour of your grief.

7. Notice if you sense any wisdom about what's next, even if it's a small step, such as eating a nourishing meal, calling a friend, journalling, or something else.

Combatting anxiety and worry

Do you worry excessively or get caught in mind chatter? Constant preoccupation with the future can provoke anxious feelings, but there are techniques to help calm them.

We all worry from time to time, but sometimes undue anxiety can become debilitating. Meditation can act as a mental brake, slowing those racing thoughts. In doing so, it gives you the space to respond consciously and compassionately to events, rather than impulsively.

An integrated approach

Given the profound interconnection between your mind and body, it can be most effective to address mental health concerns such as anxiety by integrating approaches that are both top-down (the mind influencing the body) and bottom-up (the body influencing the mind). Mindfulness-based interventions encompass strategies that can work in both directions, offering a unique approach to managing anxiety and fostering optimal mental wellbeing.

Top-down approaches:

Interrupting negative thought patterns with more productive or peaceful ones promotes relaxation and nervous system regulation. Examples include:

• labelling thoughts and emotions (see opposite).

• talking to a licensed therapist.

• social support from talking to a trusted friend.

• positive affirmations (see page 83).

• gratitude journalling (see page 87).

• mindfulness, particularly of thoughts and emotions (page 64).

Bottom-up approaches:

Body-based techniques can transform your thoughts, feelings, and brain chemistry for the better. Some examples include:

• yoga asana (see page 167).

• breathwork (also called pranayama), (see page 31).

• tai chi (see page 161).

• dance (see page 173).

• mindful movement in daily activities such as showering (see page 134).

• walking meditation (see opposite and page 144).

LABEL YOUR WORRY

Naming your distraction can help ease it. Try this top-down technique (using the mind to influence the body) seated for a silent meditation for 5–10 minutes.

1. Choose one thing as an anchor to the present moment, such as your exhales, or physical sensations such as your feet on the ground. Choose any anchor that feels right to you.

2. Notice when your mind wanders away from your chosen anchor. Each time your mind meanders, consider it an opportunity to practise coming back to the present moment.

3. Gently label the distraction with one word, such as "thinking", "planning", "evaluating", "worrying", or "feeling". Sometimes simply labelling your preoccupation enables the mind to feel like it has dealt with it, allowing us to come back to our chosen anchor.

WALKING FIX

A scattered mind, restlessness, and agitation often indicate a need to move. Simply going for a short walk is an effective bottom-up way (using the body to influence the mind) to switch your brain from anxiety to courage.

1. Stand tall and begin walking, noticing your posture.

2. Notice the sensation of your feet hitting the ground.

3. Notice your breath, which may start to naturally coordinate with the movement.

4. Notice your surroundings, allowing your eyes to scan the landscape and scene, taking in all you can see at once. (This helps, as lateral eye movement, which occurs naturally when walking and looking around, deactivates the brain's fear centre, the amygdala.)

5. When your mind wanders, come back to one of these points of awareness described in steps 1–4.

If you need more help...

Meditation can ease general worries and everyday anxieties. Still, it is not a stand-alone treatment for extreme anxiety or a clinical diagnosis. If this is what you are experiencing, it is strongly recommended to consult your medical team and work with a qualified therapist.

Managing your triggers and panic attacks

When panic takes over, it can feel like the mind is spinning out of control. It can even feel like an out-of-body experience, but meditation can help ground you.

Severe anxiety that spirals into a physical panic attack can be incredibly frightening. As a first line of defence, it can help hugely to understand what is happening.

Understanding your triggers

Coined by psychiatrist Dr Stephen Porges, the term "neuroception" refers to how your nervous system unconsciously detects whether a situation is safe, dangerous, or deadly. Conditioning from trauma or anxiety can lead to misinterpretation of the data, so our brains catastrophize situations that are actually safe. This sensitization can turn benign stimuli into triggers that can cause panic. Practising meditation over time improves your neuroception by helping you read external and internal messages better so you experience fewer false alarms.

Recognizing panic

Common signs of a panic attack include a pounding heart, difficulty breathing, dizziness, excessive sweating, shaking, chest pain, and nausea. If you experience this kind of overwhelming anxiety, you are not alone. If you or a loved one are having a panic attack (or if you think it could be something else, such as a heart attack), get medical help if needed and then use the 3-3-3 rescue technique opposite to come back down to earth.

Emotional glimmers

Coined by Deb Dana, a licensed social worker, "glimmers" are essentially the opposite of triggers. They spark joy, hope, and safety. If you experience triggers and panic attacks, it can be especially helpful to look for the glimmers in life, such as feeling the warm sunlight on your skin or a refreshing breeze, seeing a rainbow or a picture of your pet, or sharing a smile with a stranger – anything that brings you a glimpse of ease. Take a mindful moment to appreciate glimmers in your day. Also, giving the gift of a glimmer through a random act of kindness can help, too (see page 78).

THE 3-3-3 RESCUE TECHNIQUE

Next time you feel a sense of panic rising during moments of stress, such as talking to someone who triggers you or reorienting after an accident, remember the 3-3-3 rescue technique to ground you.

1. Name three things you hear around you. Try listening to sounds far away (such as street noise) and up close (such as your own voice and breath).

2. Name three things you can see around you. To yourself or out loud, say the objects, such as "door", "flowers", "my shoes", and "ceiling".

3. Move three body parts and notice your sense of touch. It can be as simple as wiggling your toes to feel your feet on the ground, touching your hands together, or getting your legs moving by walking.

Now simply notice your breath. It has likely become slower and softer. If you still need to find calm and grounding, try going for a walk (in nature, if possible) and talk to someone you trust. Humans are social creatures and connection with others is vital for the regulation of our nervous system.

THE 3-3-3 RESCUE TECHNIQUE

Following this simple technique can ground you in your surroundings, helping to calm anxiety and panic attacks.

Name 3 things you can hear

Move 3 different parts of your body

Look around and name 3 things you see

Relationships and social situations

How to deal with social situations and social anxiety isn't often taught in schools, yet these skills are crucial for our wellbeing and nervous system regulation.

It's hard enough to cope with real-world human emotions like embarrassment and awkwardness, but it's exhausting when these emotions overwhelm you and hinder your interactions with others. If you find your mind running in circles in social situations, the secret is: you don't have to catch those racing thoughts. Learning to stop and let go with mindfulness can help you process and regulate them.

ONE-MINUTE MEDITATION
For social calm

An easy and effective way to prepare yourself before a social situation or to recover from an embarrassing situation is to say "let go" as you breathe. With each inhale, say the word "let". Invite a sense of allowing. With each exhale, say the word "go". Invite a sense of release. Repeat these words as you breathe for as long as you need.

Feeling awkward

Awkwardness isn't necessarily bad; it can be charming, disarming, quirky, and authentic. Next time you feel awkward, try a healthy dose of self-acceptance by remembering that you are human. To feel less cringe amid the awkwardness, cultivate a relaxed energy through breath control (see page 51). When you are calm and present, it helps others feel at ease, replacing the cringe with connection. When engaging in small talk, slow your breathing and listen deeply.

Say you slip and fall on stage before a large audience. It's easier said than done, but if you brush it off you might be surprised at how compassionate others are. Blunders can make you more relatable. Rather than letting your thoughts descend into a shame spiral, remember: everyone has their own insecurities and fragile egos. The best medicine is to smile and laugh, but if you aren't ready to do that, try to breathe and let go (see left).

Imposter syndrome

Have you ever felt a sudden sense of doubt, questioning if you are the right person for the role you are in? Sometimes the mind plays tricks as an overcautious safety mechanism. To get past mental illusions, think of how far you have come. Would your past self be proud? Did you dream of being where you are right now? Try repeating mantras such as "I've got this", "progress, not perfection", "comparison is the thief of joy", or "the best is yet to come".

People-pleasing

Most are familiar with the fight, flight, or freeze stress responses, but there is a fourth, lesser-known option called "fawn". This is when you strive to avoid conflict by pleasing others and adapting to their needs. If this is you, the good news is that you are empathetic and can read others well, but are you good at reading yourself? Meditation can help you connect with your needs and desires and instead say "no, thank you" when something feels inauthentic. Ironically, people-pleasing doesn't make people like you more; healthy boundaries and self-respect earn respect. If you're struggling to assert yourself or battling with indecision, try the following technique.

DECIDE WHAT YOU WANT

Next time you sense you may be fawning to please others and don't know what to do, try this meditative trick to determine what you truly desire (you can also do this for an indecisive friend).

1. Grab a coin.

2. Heads means you say "yes" or keep engaging in this way. Tails means you say "no, thank you" or stop engaging in this way.

3. Flip the coin.

4. Whatever the outcome is, take a mindful moment to close your eyes and notice how it feels in your body. Do you feel relieved and more at ease or more tense? This is the intuition and wisdom of your body. It is also likely your answer.

When you are calm and present, it helps others feel at ease.

Strong emotions

Intense emotions like jealousy or envy can lead to self-destructive behaviour. Envy is different from jealousy, although both are forms of attachment. Jealousy arises when something you possess is threatened, while envy arises when you desire something that someone else has. If you find yourself feeling overwhelmed by these kinds of emotions, just *STOP*, as in the meditation to the right.

Research supports the old saying that comparison is the thief of joy. Comparison to idealistic social media images has been shown to negatively impact self-esteem and mental health. To counteract this, mindfully notice the envy and then transition it to admiration and consider practices like gratitude journalling (see page 87) or sending out loving-kindness (see page 79).

ONE-MINUTE MEDITATION
STOP: Take a mindful moment

This mindful moment from *A Mindfulness-Based Stress Reduction Workbook* by Bob Stahl and Elisha Goldstein creates space between the stimulus and response, so you can react thoughtfully by being curious rather than accusatory. It will help you recognize if you need to reach out to a loved one or if you need space to process what has happened and practise a longer meditation for clarity.

Stop.

Take several slow breaths.

Observe what's coming up. What do you feel in your body?

Proceed with appropriate action (or inaction) with awareness.

Being ghosted

In these moments, when someone you like is not responding, shift your focus to those who choose to be in your life. Think of three people you are grateful for and imagine them smiling and well. Put this into action by sending a message to let them know why or how much you appreciate them.

FOMO

In the age of social media highlights, FOMO (fear of missing out) thrives as we constantly compare our lives to those of others. Over time, practising meditation will dissolve FOMO as you become more content with what is. Daily mindfulness sparks curiosity and infinite interest in the present moment, replacing boredom and zombie scrolling. Meditation transforms FOMO to JOMO (joy of missing out) as "feel-good" chemicals and hormones become balanced, and you learn to find joy in simplicity.

Meditation can help you connect with your needs and desires.

Improve concentration and focus

Just as you need to warm up before running a race, your mind craves a warm-up before a bout of intense focus for work, study, or challenges like public speaking. Meditation is known as a boot camp for your focus.

Through practice, you develop stronger mental muscles to resist distractions and come back to the present. Working in engaged sprints followed by meditative breaks could really improve your productivity. Meditation and breathing practices can act as a dynamic warm-up before a work session or as strategic breaks to refocus.

Find a new focus

The third eye, or ajna chakra, is deemed mystical in yoga. It is said that closing your eyes and directing your attention to the area between your eyebrows can help you open an invisible third eye for greater wisdom, intuition, and awareness. Although there is no anatomical third eye, meditation is most known for activating a part of the brain that sits behind your forehead called the prefrontal cortex. This area is responsible for concentrating on a task, complex cognition, and resisting distractions.

CONCENTRATION MEDITATION

A common concentration technique is simply to focus on the third eye as you sit and breathe for several minutes. Feel free to put on some strategic sounds (see page 137) to enhance your practice.

1. Take several slow, deep breaths.

2. Bring your awareness and your gaze to the area between your eyebrows. If at any point it feels forced, relax your eye muscles and simply maintain your awareness of the third eye. If comfortable, close your eyes.

3. Softly focus on the area for five minutes before a work session or as a short break.

The good kind of stress

When you are about to go on stage or perhaps take the mic in a work presentation, do you feel sweaty, get flushed, have a dry mouth, or taste metal? Before taking an exam, does your breathing quicken? These are signs of your body activating your stress response or sympathetic nervous system (see page 50). But stress is bad, right? Actually, stress isn't always bad. In fact, there are two types of stress: distress (what we normally think of as "stress") and eustress (beneficial stress that motivates us). Coming from the same root as the word euphoria ("eu" meaning good), eustress has been shown to induce different physiological changes to distress, including less strain on your cardiovascular system and a burst of the love hormone oxytocin, which helps heal damage to your heart. Meditation techniques can channel distress into eustress to help you approach whatever challenge or task you face with a clear, calm mind that is ready to focus. Try the practices on the following page.

POSITIVE STRESS

Beneficial stress (such as an engaging work project, inspired creative performance, or an act of courage) is known as eustress and sparks resilience.

NEGATIVE STRESS

Real or imagined stress, or distress (such as worrying about a deadline or the outcome of a performance or test) puts a load on your tissues and systems.

ALTERNATE NOSTRIL BREATHING

Often used in yoga practice, alternate nostril breathing can help you feel centred, calm, and balanced – ideal for focus.

1. Look at your right hand (this can be done with the right or left hand, but these instructions are for the right hand). Bring your thumb towards your ring finger. These are the two fingers you are going to use to block your nostrils.

2. Cover your right nostril with your thumb.

3. Slowly exhale and then inhale through your left nostril for three counts each, or whatever is comfortable for you.

4. Switch to cover your left nostril with your ring finger and open the right nostril.

5. Exhale and then inhale through your right nostril.

6. Switch nostrils again and exhale and inhale. Alternate for several minutes. Just remember: exhale, inhale, switch.

(If this isn't comfortable for your hands, try it hands-free by simply imagining that your nostrils are blocked. Feel the breath flow mostly through one nostril first, then the other.)

ALTERNATE NOSTRIL BREATHING

Use the thumb to cover one nostril as you exhale and inhale.

Switch and use the ring finger to cover the other nostril as you exhale and inhale.

RISE AND THRIVE
WHEN UNDER PRESSURE

Next time you need to perform optimally, whether it be public speaking or an exam, transform distress into eustress and fear into courage. Prior to stepping on stage or taking a test, recognize, reframe, and ground to focus on the task.

1. Recognize stress: First, simply notice the symptoms of stress in your body. Feel how it shows up for you.

2. Reframe stress: This is your body rising to the demand. Your pounding heart energizes you, and stress hormones have the side effect of making you highly alert. What you are doing is important, and your body is here to help you succeed.

3. Ground down to rise up: Often, the breath is shallow and in the chest when we are stressed, so try to bring your breath down, allowing your abdomen to move with it. You can also bring your awareness down to feel your feet on the ground. Grounding down can help us rise up to face challenges with courage.

Taking a technology break

Technology solves problems but, at times, it causes them, too. Screen time can be distracting, disruptive, and addictive, so occasionally it's good for us to switch off.

The digital world is constantly bombarding us with content, but the human brain is not meant to process so much information in a rapid-fire way. It is built for slow, contextualized changes with the movement of the eyes – seeing the sky, then a hut, then a tree, for example – but now the context flicks from politics to kittens to an image of your school heartbreak smiling with their new love. It can be overwhelming, plus exposure to blue screen light can disrupt our circadian rhythm (see page 102), so take a break from scrolling and slow down with these mini meditations.

ONE-MINUTE MEDITATION
Avoiding message regret

Ever feel regret after pressing send? Before you send a message: pause, close your eyes or look away from the screen, and take three deep breaths. When you are done, feel in your body if it is time to press send. If needed, rewrite or walk away to get in the right headspace.

Tech addict?

Apps are designed to be addictive and to entice you to engage. Your brain makes a powerful chemical called dopamine, which is especially released in anticipation of momentary pleasure. From the hopes of a few likes on your social media post to a gambling win, dopamine keeps you coming back for more – even when it's not good for you. Have some compassion for yourself. If you tap some apps more often than desired, practising meditation and being mindful throughout your day can help you with the first step: recognizing when you have a problem.

Tech frustrations

Has searching for a link made you late for a video call? Has your screen frozen at the worst time? Sometimes we need a meditation (or at least a meditative moment) to **Recognize**, **Reframe**, and **Repeat** to keep us calm when technology gets frustrating.

Recognize

Notice any thoughts, such as "I am bad at technology" or "This always happens to me." Remember that thoughts are not facts, and everyone has to deal with tech issues. Also, recognize when you need to take a break and walk away. Here are two healthy choices amid the tech frustration:

Reframe and repeat

Transform self-critical thoughts to something like "I am learning technology" or "I can face this challenge." Choose something that feels true and constructive to you. The more you recognize thinking patterns that are unhelpful, the quicker you get at stopping them. Consider repeating your new thought several times so it becomes a mantra.

Rest and return

You may need to walk away and take a break, especially if it is late or you are tired. Try any of the meditations in this section or a walking meditation (see page 144). Return with a fresh mind to tackle the problem. It's funny how sometimes a restart or unplug is literally what fixes a tech issue and, metaphorically, is what we need, too.

SCREEN-BREAK YOGA

Take screen breaks with these eye exercises, ending in a short, warming meditation to relax your eye muscles.

1. Blink several times.

2. Look at something far away (and away from the screen), allowing your vision to blur for a few moments.

3. Look at something up close, like the tip of your nose.

4. Look left, right, up, and down. Then roll your eyes clockwise and counterclockwise.

5. Rub your hands together to generate warmth, then cup your hands and hover them over your eyes for at least five breaths (if you wear glasses, take them off first). Feel the warmth of your hands relax the muscles around your eyes.

BREAK FROM ZOMBIE SCROLLING

Social media is designed to keep you infinitely scrolling or swiping, but don't feed into it. If you notice yourself scrolling mindlessly, zombie-like, try this:

1. Get your hands off the screen. Put your hands on your lap or on your heart. (Heck, sit on your hands if needed!)

2. Readjust your posture. Simply sitting up tall can break the zombie spell. It can alleviate some pain, too, since the forward head position can overwork and strain your neck and shoulder muscles.

3. Inquire internally. What would be nourishing right now? A walk? Winding down for bed? An audio meditation? Sitting in silence?

Put your phone aside and reconnect with your mind and body to break the spell of zombie scrolling.

Doom scrolling

The excessive consumption of news, which tends to be negatively skewed to generate more views, can lead to a sense of doom. It isn't your fault. Humans are neurologically wired to anticipate and prevent danger. Scanning for threats is a primal skill that serves us when needed. But reading about events on the other side of the world leaves us feeling helpless and overwhelmed. So, become an alchemist of feelings with this golden nugget from the Tibetan Buddhist technique of Tonglen, which is the Tibetan term for giving and taking:

Inhale. Acknowledge your present feelings, such as frustration, pain at the suffering of others, darkness...

Exhale. Imagine yourself exuding compassion, loving-kindness, and light...

Repeat this visualization for several slow breaths or for as long as you need.

Fight fatigue and recuperate

The modern world is a hectic place. As we juggle work, life administration, travel, family, and social life, most of us are in an exhausting tailspin much of the time. Somehow, amid all this, we can find time to re-energize and recharge.

One vital skill that meditation teaches us is how to know intuitively when it is OK to push through it and when it is best to rest through it. When you have a deadline, you may need to fight the fatigue with the energizing practices opposite left, but when you feel burnt out, try the techniques opposite right to rejuvenate yourself.

And when it feels like it's all just too much, try the meditation on this page to give yourself a break.

Envision thoughts like soap bubbles slowly floating away into an open blue sky.

MEDITATION TO TAKE THE LOAD OFF

Sometimes it can feel like the weight of the world is on your shoulders. Take about 10 minutes to lighten the load and slow down with this visualization.

1. Lie down and put your feet up. You can lie on a sofa with pillows or cushions elevating your legs, or on the floor with your calves resting on the seat of any chair.

2. Notice the speed and types of thoughts popping up.

3. Envision thoughts like soap bubbles slowly floating away into an open blue sky. They effortlessly drift by – even spontaneously pop – as you return to a natural resting place in the present moment.

Practices to energize

Yoga: *Try back bends and strong standing poses or sun salutations, which are flowing movements synchronized with the breath that transition from standing to kneeling.*
Breathwork: *Upside-down triangle breathing, holding the breath after the inhale:*
· *Follow this image with whatever equal breath count is comfortable for you (2, 3, 4, 5, 6, or 7 seconds).*

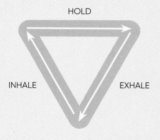

HOLD

INHALE   EXHALE

Breathwork: *Right-nostril breathing is associated with an increase in sympathetic nervous system activity, giving you more energy. Here's how to practise it:*
· *Cover your left nostril.*
· *Try practising with your eyes open to encourage alertness.*
· *Focus awareness on the inhales to further energize yourself.*
· *Take at least 10 slow, even breaths through your right nostril, or do the upside-down triangle breathing technique (above) through your right nostril.*
Meditation: *Sit tall and shift your gaze slightly upwards towards your third eye (see page 66) or try a walking meditation (see page 144).*

Practices to recuperate

Yoga: *Try forward folds and poses on the ground or restorative yoga, which uses pillows or cushions and other props for support in longer-held poses.*
Breathwork: *Triangle breathing, holding the breath after the exhale:*
· *Follow this image using whatever equal breath count is most comfortable for you (2, 3, 4, 5, 6, or 7 seconds).*

INHALE   EXHALE

HOLD

Breathwork: *Left-nostril breathing is associated with an increase in parasympathetic nervous system activity, relaxing you. Here's how to practise it:*
· *Cover your right nostril.*
· *Try practising with your eyes closed, if comfortable, to limit distractions.*
· *Focus awareness on the exhales to encourage a sense of release.*
· *Take at least 10 slow breaths through your left nostril or enhance the effects by incorporating the triangle breathing technique (above).*
Meditation: *Lie down with pillows and blankets and try a yoga nidra (see page 170) or loving-kindness meditation (see page 79).*

Boost your memory

Forgetting your keys and people's names more often? Many of us accept that memory inevitably declines with age, but it is possible to improve it at any age. By enhancing present-moment awareness and reducing the burden of stress through meditation, memory can be sharpened.

It is true that the area of the brain associated with memory – the hippocampus – tends to shrink as we get older and with conditions like chronic pain, depression, and trauma. However, this process is reversible.

Meditation and mindfulness programmes have been shown to increase the size of the hippocampus. In turn, this leads to better memory recall, enhanced working memory, and improved focus and cognition in both healthy individuals and people with cognitive decline.

Fighting dementia

While new medications and treatments to help with dementia symptoms are being developed, there is currently no miraculous cure for the condition. Emerging research, however, shows that meditation and mindfulness training can slow its progression and help improve quality of life. Clinical trials using Kirtan Kriya meditation (see opposite) – a repetitive chanting exercise from the Kundalini tradition, accompanied by specific hand movements and singing – have shown promising results in Alzheimer's disease, counteracting the harmful effects of chronic stress on the mind and, in some cases, reversing memory loss. With such results, meditation can be considered a promising complementary therapy alongside medical care for dementia and related diseases. Plus, regular practice can provide protective mechanisms to help keep your brain healthy, especially as you age.

MEMORY MEDITATION

Known as Kirtan Kriya, this 12-minute meditation can be practised anytime, but it is recommended in the morning. It can be done alone or in a group. The coordination and repetition involved help boost brain activity and improve focus. You can read through and close your eyes as you get the hang of it, or practise with a recording at meditationfortherealworld.com/memory.

1. Sit tall in a chair or on the floor.

2. Place your hands on your thighs with palms facing up.

3. On both hands at the same time: touch your thumbs to your **index fingers**, repeating out loud the word **"Saa"**; touch your thumbs to your **middle fingers**, repeating the word **"Taa"**; touch your thumbs to your **ring fingers**, repeating the word **"Naa"**; touch your thumbs to your **little fingers**, repeating the word **"Maa"**. (If you can't touch them, move the fingers as much as possible and visualize them touching instead.)

4. Sing the mantra "Saa Taa Naa Maa" in the tune of the first four notes of the nursery rhyme "Mary Had a Little Lamb".

5. Feel free to use a timer to repeat this exercise using the following pattern: sing the mantra **out loud** for two minutes to begin; **whisper** it for two minutes; repeat it **silently** for four minutes; **whisper** it for two minutes; sing it **out loud** for two minutes to finish.

6. Once you get comfortable with it, you can visualize the sound entering from the crown of your head and leaving out of your third eye between your brows, while closing your eyes.

THE KIRTAN KRIYA MEDITATION TECHNIQUE

The four hand positions, or mudras, repeated in Kirtan Kriya cultivate focus.

SAA

TAA

NAA

MAA

Compassion and connection with others

Compassion and kindness are keystones of meditation; they not only support others, but are also good for your own wellbeing.

It's been shown that people who do volunteer work tend to live longer, and that performing random acts of kindness leads to happiness that lasts for weeks. Doing good for others activates your brain's pleasure and reward centres, giving you a boost of endorphins and what scientists call the "helper's high".

ONE-MINUTE REFLECTION
Random acts of kindness

Reflect: How did you bring a smile to someone's face today? Imagine them smiling and at ease. Take 30 seconds of stillness and notice how you feel.

Reflect: What act of kindness will you do today? Now do it. It can be as small as texting a thank-you to someone you appreciate or calling a lonely grandparent. Observe how you feel in your body for another mini meditation afterwards.

Be kind to yourself first

For many, being kind to ourselves is challenging, especially if you struggle with perfectionism. Holding yourself to unrealistic standards can lead to excessive criticism of yourself (and others) and can take a toll on your mental health. But here's the thing: practising self-compassion takes the edge off.

Rephrase negative self-talk using kinder words, as you would speak to a dear friend or child. When sending loving-kindness to yourself, picture yourself as a child. Then, after extending kindness to others, repeat Step 2 of the loving-kindness meditation and give yourself some extra love. You might find this easier after you have tried practising compassion for others.

LOVING-KINDNESS (METTA) MEDITATION

Do you need to find some "loving-kindness" for yourself today, or for others? You can use this meditation at any time to give yourself compassion; for example, when feeling anger, embarrassment, or when feeling ill. It will especially help you feel more connected and patient with others.

1. Find a comfortable position, seated or lying down, and take a few moments to breathe slowly to settle your energy.

2. Repeat these phrases (or some of your own) to direct loving-kindness to yourself while visualizing a comforting light radiating from your body:

> *"May I be safe."*
> *"May I be healthy."*
> *"May I be joyful."*
> *"May I be free from suffering."*
> *"May I be at ease."*

To practise loving-kindness towards others, you will need to envision different people. Let's decide who first:

An admired person: Reflect on an individual (or group) you respect – someone you are grateful to for helping you either directly or through inspiration.

A loved one: Envisage a beloved person (or group) who effortlessly evokes positive feelings for you. Consider who you deeply appreciate right now – someone who makes you smile.

A stranger: Choose a neutral stranger, such as the person in front of you in a shop queue.

A difficult person: Identify someone (or a group) who is moderately challenging to you – for example, an irritating workmate or the person who cut in front of you during your morning commute.

All beings and life: Widen your awareness to envision all people, animals, plants, and the earth as a whole.

Now you are ready to practise.

1. Get comfortable, seated or lying down, and as before, take a few moments to breathe slowly to settle your energy.

2. Repeat the following for each of the people (or groups) identified. Visualize them smiling and filled with light as you repeat the words:

> *"May they be safe."*
> *"May they be healthy."*
> *"May they be joyful."*
> *"May they be free from suffering."*
> *"May they be at ease."*

Recovering from trauma

Healing from trauma is a non-linear journey. Unresolved trauma can trap you in cycles of ruminating on past events or rehearsing your response to potential danger in the future. Meditation gets you out of your head and into what's happening now, enabling your nervous system to more accurately interpret your body signals and environment.

Meditation teaches that we are not defined by our thoughts, emotions, or the events that have occurred in our lives. The philosophies that inform meditation say that nobody is broken or needs to be fixed. You are whole, and there is an inner peace within you (and everyone) that just needs to be revealed. Imagine a light covered with dust and gunk; meditation can help clean the light so it shines again.

Trauma and the brain

There are common changes to the brain after trauma. The fear centre (amygdala) is in overdrive, which can turn benign stimuli into triggers. The memory centre (hippocampus) is degraded, leading to brain fog. Areas of the brain involved in processing physical sensations are affected, which can make even a light touch painful. The prefrontal cortex is also degraded, making it hard to regulate emotions in everyday life. Alterations in neural circuitry can lead to sensory and emotional overwhelm.

The good news is that meditation and mindful movement practices can reverse the maladaptive brain changes from trauma through the nervous system's ability to adapt its responses due to experience (known as neuroplasticity). These practices have been shown to aid recovery from trauma and post-traumatic stress disorder (PTSD), while the philosophy behind meditation supports personal growth.

In addition to PTSD, there is also a phenomenon called post-traumatic growth (PTG). Just as challenging your muscles in a hard workout leads to initial micro-tears on the surface that heal to make the muscles stronger and more capable, people who experience trauma report strength from personal growth, profound realizations, and transformations.

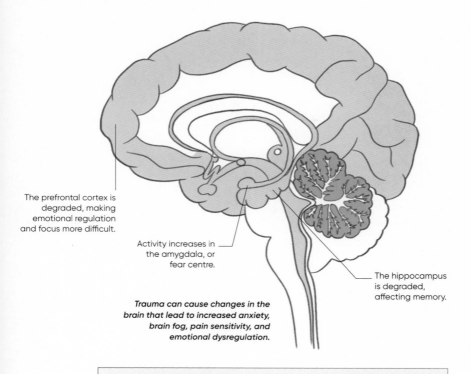

The prefrontal cortex is degraded, making emotional regulation and focus more difficult.

Activity increases in the amygdala, or fear centre.

The hippocampus is degraded, affecting memory.

Trauma can cause changes in the brain that lead to increased anxiety, brain fog, pain sensitivity, and emotional dysregulation.

Seek help

Remember that meditation is one part of an integrative health approach and is not sufficient by itself for treating serious mental health conditions. Seek help from mental health professionals and develop a support system. It will also be helpful to find a meditation class or teacher to personalize your practice. You don't have to do this alone – and nor should you.

Meditating through trauma

If you are reading this, you may be looking for ways to feel soothed as you go through your experiences. Any time that you can take for yourself, to rest and recover, is important.

Self-compassion: *Healing and growth is not a straight path. Go easy on yourself.*

Acknowledge your body: *Remember that issues are stored in your tissues. A typical response to trauma is to disassociate from the body. Trauma can also show up as physical pain or discomfort, such as tightness in the chest or digestive issues. Practices like body scans can be helpful to get you back in touch with your body, but* always stay in your comfort zone and feel free to visualize a safe place if needed (see opposite left).

Safe space: *Consider your meditation cushion, yoga mat, or area where you are meditating as your safe place. The practice is yours. Find any position that is comfortable, and remember that closing your eyes is always optional – feel free to keep your eyes open with a soft gaze if you prefer. Also, anytime you need, you can visualize that you are somewhere that feels safe – like at the ocean or with a beloved puppy.*

Stay in your comfort zone: *Recognize that not all meditation and breathing techniques will feel relaxing or OK to you. Every part of the practice is your choice to do or not.*

Trauma triggers

If you ever feel triggered or overwhelmed, or sense a panic attack coming on, seek support from a loved one, medical professional, and licensed therapist whenever possible.

VISUALIZING A SAFE PLACE

Imagining a safe place that you can mentally visit whenever you need to can be very therapeutic. It promotes feelings of peace and reassurance in place of agitation and fear. You can do this anywhere or anytime when your feelings become overwhelming.

1. Where and when do you feel most at ease?

2. Visualize a real or imagined place that is safe and comfortable.

3. Perhaps you are in nature, with a loved one, in your favourite cosy chair, or even floating on a cloud. Maybe you have been to this place or it's a place you've always wanted to visit. Whatever place that comes to mind is right.

4. Recruit all your senses to imagine being there.

5. What do you see? Hear? Smell? Taste? Physically feel?

6. Notice how your body and breath respond to this visualization.

7. Rest in this awareness for as long as you would like.

Remember that you can come back to this safe oasis anytime you need throughout your day or to help you fall asleep at night. The more you practise, the easier it will be to cultivate a sense of safety.

AFFIRMATIONS FOR TRAUMA PROCESSING

Positive affirmations are empowering to use through everyday activities whenever you need them or in a seated mantra meditation. Each time you repeat your chosen affirmations, you are rewiring your brain for healthier thinking patterns.

1. Repeat any of these phrases as a mantra for several breaths or several minutes, or just remind yourself during the day. Choose one from the list or create one that feels right in your body. You may want to write it somewhere you can see it as a reminder.

> *"I am safe."*
> *"I am worthy."*
> *"I deserve to be loved."*
> *"I am loved."*
> *"I am not alone."*
> *"What happened does not define me."*
> *"I have choices."*
> *"I am not defined by an event."*
> *"I give myself permission to heal."*

Life challenges

Whether you are going home for the holidays, moving house, attending a family reunion, or even getting married, your chill will likely be challenged by these potentially stressful events – even if you're excited about them!

Life challenges build resilience. When you exercise, you are, in essence, tearing muscle fibres, but as they heal they build back stronger. In the same way, obstacles in life provide an opportunity for personal growth. It's likely that the most inspirational and influential people you know have been through significant adversities that made them the person you now admire.

There is a concept in biology called hormesis, which is the adaptive response of cells and organisms to stress. Basically, it means that what doesn't kill you makes you stronger, and it is happening at a cellular level. Likewise, meditation and breathwork can help you get through tough times and grow stronger internally.

Building resilience

Regular meditation practice develops resilience by building new neural pathways, helping you to bounce back from stress. When learning football, you practise drills with a buddy. You build skills in a safe setting where you can make lots of mistakes, not in the heat of the big game. Similarly, when you sit down to meditate, you may get frustrated when your mind wanders, especially when you are thinking about something stressful. You may notice your heart racing and your chest tightening. But that's OK because you can redirect yourself to the present, which builds the skill of emotional regulation.

You are also developing the skill of switching physiological states purposefully and quickly. This is like training for your mind. The next time a family member says something that triggers you, for example, or there is a delay in the home-buying process, you may notice your heart pounding, but you have built the skill to regulate your nervous system in the heat of the moment. We can't control all stressors, but we can learn to control our responses to them. It takes practice, and this is why we call meditation a practice.

Transition moments

Weddings, memorials, break-ups, and divorces often represent a time of significant change. Transitions can be the hardest times of life but also the most transformational. If you find yourself in one of these challenging transition moments, take a moment to pause and then try this:

Take several deep breaths. Like a snow globe, all shaken up, imagine your thoughts and energy settling down with each long exhale.

Physically feel your body as your energy settles for 10 slow breaths, following this figure-of-eight visual:

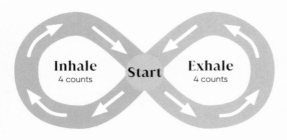

Consider who you are grateful for right now. If it's comfortable, close your eyes for several slow breaths as you visualize those people.

EMERGENCY CALM FIX

You can practise this particular technique in the heat of the moment, when you need to calm down. You can also try it now so you know what to do in those life-challenging moments. Square breathing, or box breathing, is so-called because the four stages of the breath last for the same count, like the four sides of a square or box. It's a technique used by US Navy SEALs during extremely high-pressure situations. Yes, you can learn a technique that has helped people endure the stress of wartime raids to better face the stress of visiting your parents!

1. Inhale for four seconds. If four counts are uncomfortable, try the exercise with three.

2. Hold the breath for four seconds.

3. Exhale for four seconds.

4. Hold that breath for four seconds. Repeat a few times until you feel calmer.

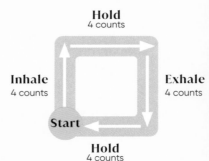

GRATITUDE JOURNAL

During challenging times, it can help to shift your focus to gratitude. Studies show that counting your blessings in a daily (or sometimes just weekly) journal entry can notably improve sleep, healthy habits, and mental health. You can do this regularly, or whenever you need a boost of positivity. Practising gratitude makes you more grateful, creating a positive loop. A white paper called "The Science of Gratitude" released by the Greater Good Science Center outlines the robust research on how gratitude can improve your wellbeing. Try some of the most promising methods used in the research it summarizes here:

1. List three to five things you are grateful for. This can include people, events, opportunities, or whatever comes to mind.

2. Try to think of a cause for each thing you are grateful for, if there is one. Write it down.

3. Write a positive gratitude message or letter to at least one person you feel you haven't properly thanked. Send it.

4. After you complete any or all of these journalling exercises, set a timer for five minutes and simply focus on how you feel. Notice how you feel physically, emotionally, and perhaps spiritually. With each exhale, relax further into that feeling.

Regular meditation practice develops resilience by building new neural pathways, helping you to bounce back from stress.

Meditating from an early age

In school, we were taught reading, writing, and arithmetic, but somehow the curriculum did not include how to stay happy and healthy.

Rates of child and teen anxiety and depression are on the rise across the globe. Meditation and mindfulness programmes have been shown to help children manage stress, attention, anxiety, depression, and pain. These programmes are now being integrated into schools and clinical practices because they show improvements in the children's social and emotional learning– an area of growing interest in childhood education.

The developing brains of young people are particularly responsive to learning meditation and mindfulness practices, making it a promising intervention for improving cognition and emotional regulation. One research review showed that meditation improved academic performance, including greater focus, better cognitive functioning and flexibility, a boost in working memory, and faster information processing. Meditation and yoga have also been shown to help children with attention deficit hyperactivity disorder (ADHD) to pay attention better, while reducing their hyperactivity and impulsive behaviours. Just one session led to improved thinking and problem-solving. Plus, when parents and children with ADHD learn meditation, their family relationships improve.

From toddlers to teens

Teaching young children to meditate may feel like a ridiculous endeavour, since it can be hard to get them to stay still for a minute. However, even toddlers can learn simple breathing techniques that have immediate effects on how they feel. Sitting quietly doesn't have to be a "time out" or punishment; it can be quality time. Since children model their behaviour on that of their parents, learning together can be very effective.

Meditations for teens often look similar to those for adults, making any practice in this book a valuable resource for them. For younger children, shapes, games, and stories are often incorporated to make it fun, as on page 91.

Learning how to deal with emotions

Students who were taught how to meditate at school told researchers they felt more optimism, self-acceptance, and positive emotions. They also tended to take better care of their health and engage in more pro-social behaviours (like helping others) and fewer antisocial ones (like anger). One student reported, "If I meditate, I feel calm and feel like I don't have to argue with anybody." Another student reported, "It's made me a calm person and easier to talk to, and [I] listen to other people."

RAIN TECHNIQUE

When kids feel overwhelmed, it can be helpful for them to learn about how the emotions work. The RAIN technique (Recognize, Accept, Investigate, Non-identify) was originally developed by meditation teacher Michele McDonald and below it is adapted for kids. You could use it to guide a child through tantrums or difficult emotions. Remember the steps using the acronym:

1. Recognize that you are feeling a big emotion right now and try to identify it. Naming our emotions helps us feel better and act better. When it comes to big emotions, sometimes we need to name it to tame it.

2. Accept the emotion just as it is. Remember that emotions are natural and everyone feels them. Rather than stopping the emotion, accept it. Sometimes we have to feel it to heal it.

3. Investigate what you are feeling with curiosity. Notice how your body feels. What does it feel like? (Tingling? Tight? Warm? Like fire? Like ice? Rising? Sinking? Big? Small?) Where do you feel it in your body? (Your head? Chest? Belly? Everywhere?)

4. Nurture it. Remember it's not you. *Help your child to move forward by saying: remember that just because you are feeling [angry, sad, etc....] it doesn't mean you are a bad or [angry, sad, etc....] person. It is not your identity or who you are [this is a key concept in mindfulness called "non-identification"].*

Encourage your child to nurture their feelings with kindness and compassion for themselves and others. Now ask your child, what could you do to soothe yourself? Suggest asking for a hug, saying something nice to yourself or someone you love, or taking deep breaths using the technique below.

RAINBOW BREATHING

Use the image of a rainbow to teach children how to use meditative breathing to calm themselves and regain control when they are feeling overwhelmed or panicked. Ask your child to draw a rainbow, or use a beautiful photo or artwork.

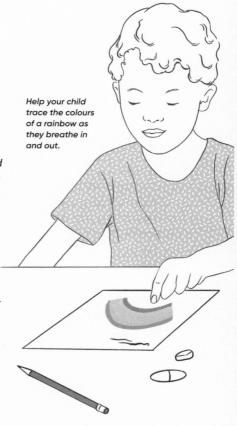

Help your child trace the colours of a rainbow as they breathe in and out.

1. Place your finger at the bottom of the purple arc in the rainbow.

2. Breathe in as you trace your finger over the purple arc.

3. Place your finger on the blue arc.

4. Breathe out as you trace your finger over the blue arc.

5. Continue through all the colours of the rainbow, making your breaths longer as the coloured arcs get longer.

Tap in to creativity

Whether it's for work or pleasure or problem-solving, human beings are all creative in some way, but with so much going on in our lives and so many distractions crowding in on us, the creative mindset can be hard to tap in to.

If you would like to become more creative, or you have a creative "block" right now, meditation can help. This could be in a writing project, creating something visual, or needing a solution in some part of your life. Meditation techniques such as those explained below encourage flexibility and fluency in creative problem-solving. Taking time to meditate can unlock ideas and get those creative juices flowing.

The principles of creative meditation

The three-part meditation opposite is a great warm-up to proactively cultivate the right vibe to get creating. Here are the processes behind the practice:

1. Be aware of sensation: When you do the meditation opposite, you will first become aware of physical sensations in your hands. They are filled with a huge number of sensory receptors for such a small area, making them excellent body parts to focus on. Since the left side of your brain controls the right side of your body and vice versa, shifting attention back and forth between hands builds connectivity bridges between the brain hemispheres.

2. Explore opposites: Next, you'll explore opposite feelings and ideas (like hot and cold or expansion and contraction). This helps you recognize that things are not simply black or white, or good or bad; they can be both simultaneously. Also, the exercise emphasizes how the only thing that doesn't change is the fact that everything changes. There is no need to worry if you are feeling stuck because these states are everchanging (and perhaps even illusions). You can also feel open, inviting creativity to flow.

3. Open-monitoring: Last, you will play with a technique called open-monitoring, where you open your awareness to whatever arises in the present moment, noticing thoughts and sensations and letting them go. Scientists have found this can enhance the divergent thinking indicative of creativity.

MEDITATION FOR CREATIVITY

Take 10–20 minutes to go through these instructions. Read each step, then close your eyes and try it.

1. Notice the palms of your hands. Bring your attention to your left hand and feel it fully. **Notice** all the flowing sensations and vibrations in that hand. Then bring your attention to your right hand and feel it fully. **Notice** your right hand holding these sensations. Go back to feeling your left hand for a few moments, then your right hand. **Repeat**, going back and forth, increasing the speed. Then, feel both hands simultaneously for several breaths.

2. Recruit your imagination to go a bit more conceptual now. **Invite** a feeling of being expansive, open, infinite, and boundless. **Feel** expansive like the sky for several moments. **Invite** a feeling of being constricted, closed, small, and confined. How does this feel in your body? What happens to your breath? Go back to feeling expansive/open for a few moments, then constricted/closed for a few moments, increasing the speed. Then, **play** with feeling both simultaneously. What happens to your thoughts, feelings, breath, and body when you invite both?

3. Now, expand your consciousness and rest in open awareness. Allow an open mind to any thoughts or sensations. Welcome whatever arises and accept it without judgement. Allow your mind to do as it pleases for several minutes until you are ready to create.

Meditating with others

Meditation is often viewed as a solitary practice. However, humans are social animals. We thrive in groups and in a variety of partnerships – from lovers to friends to beloved pets.

When we meditate with others, especially a loved one, a magical process called co-regulation occurs naturally. This means that by simply being near a person who senses your distress and "just gets you", you both tend to regulate your emotions better than you would do alone.

Co-regulation

When dealing with the stresses of life, you are wired to reach out to others for support. The biological process of co-regulation is influenced by the vagus nerve and mirror neurons. Social connection can activate the mirror neurons in the brain, which prompts you to emulate the body positioning and moods of others around you. Whether you are meditating with a significant other or imitating the movements of a yoga teacher in class, activation of these pro-social networks tends to evoke empathy, connection, and ease.

When you connect with others, it sends cues of safety through a part of the vagus nerve involved in social connection (the ventral vagus), which slows your heart rate, lowers your blood pressure, and puts you in a state of calm, especially when meditating with others. (Sometimes, when we are being social, it is more playful and active. Learn more about that on page 174.)

Laughter yoga

This may sound silly, but laughter therapies have been shown to help reduce anxiety and depression symptoms and improve sleep. Laughing releases endorphins. This is no joke – even simulated laughter seems to work. So let laughter flow freely with others or even join a laughter yoga group, which often incorporates playful laughter exercises, breathwork, stretches, and meditation techniques.

The power of a hug

Hugs reduce the stress hormone cortisol and increase oxytocin, also known as "the cuddle hormone" or "love hormone". This deepens our connection and bond with others. Human contact through hugs and massage therapy has been shown to reduce loneliness and could even protect you from getting sick. Similar results have been found with pets.

CONSCIOUS CONTACT MEDITATION

Enhance your meditation by practising with your pet in your lap or sitting back to back (or knee to knee) with a loved one.

1. Take a moment to settle and allow both partners to get comfortable.

2. Rest your awareness on the point of contact with the person or pet you are connecting with. Imagine you are sending your breath to those points of contact.

3. Become aware of their breath, pulse, or anything else you feel.

4. If your mind wanders, come back to feeling the points of contact.

5. Rest together for as long as is comfortable. In time, you may notice your internal rhythms begin to synchronize.

Meditating with another person, or with a pet, can enhance your practice through the process of co-regulation.

CHAPTER 3

MEDITATION FOR A HEALTHY BODY

Get out of your head and into your body. This chapter introduces meditations that fine-tune your awareness to help you become a more attentive listener to your body's requests and innate wisdom. Whether it's whispering or screaming, your body is speaking to you, and it's likely asking you to chill out.

Just as one medicine cannot treat all diseases, so one meditation technique isn't perfect for everybody in every circumstance. In this chapter, we'll explore targeted techniques to improve sleep, enhance immunity, lower blood pressure, and ease many types of pain and discomfort, including arthritis, back pain, PMS, digestive upset, and headaches. You'll even find practices you can do at the doctor's office or post-procedure to support recovery.

Meditating complements your regular healthcare and medical treatments, enhancing their effects and helping you recover more quickly. Each time you meditate, you are investing in your health.

Struggling with sleep?

Better sleep can transform your physical and mental health. Whether your mind is spinning before bed or you awaken during the night, meditation can help.

A good night's sleep really is the foundation for calm, clear thinking. You may also notice memory enhancement, improved mood, less pain, a faster metabolism, and fewer sugar cravings. But sleep disturbance is common, with causes ranging from pain and anxiety to lifestyle choices. Meditation has been shown to help with many of these issues. Plus, being mindful can help you connect how your behaviours impact on your sleep. Which of the common causes of sleep issues below affect you?

Common causes of sleep problems

- Pain, stress, and anxiety
- Caffeine intake, alcohol, and drugs
- Smoking and nicotine
- Changing sleep time and duration
- Eating within 2–3 hours before bed
- Drinking water before bed, leading to a midnight bathroom break
- Inadequate exercise or high-intensity exercise before bed
- A suboptimal sleep environment (e.g. too hot, too loud)
- Lack of natural daylight
- Artificial light, such as blue screen light, close to your bed

Research shows meditation can help

Meditation has been shown to improve sleep quality in a number of studies. In one randomized controlled trial published in *JAMA Internal Medicine*, just six weekly sessions of mindfulness meditation training with 5–20 minutes of daily practice led to meaningful reductions in insomnia, fatigue, depression, and brain fog. The mindfulness outcomes were superior to those of the control group enrolled in a sleep hygiene education programme, which involves maintaining a good sleep environment and daily routine to promote high-quality sleep.

There are several techniques that can help you fall asleep, such as the bee breath (see page 113), yoga nidra (see page 170), and elongated exhales (see page 51). For a natural muscle relaxant, you can practise the progressive muscle relaxation (PMR) technique on the following few pages as part of your wind-down routine to fall asleep with more ease.

Relax your body, calm your mind

Progressive muscle relaxation (PMR) is a systematic way of intentionally engaging and releasing your muscles to release tension. You may have done it at the end of your yoga practice while in the final relaxation pose, or as part of a yoga nidra.

To practise, you sequentially squeeze and release each body part from head to toe (or toe to head). Right away, this distracts you from racing thoughts to calm your mind. It also strategically teaches your nervous system the difference between tension and relaxation, especially by highlighting body parts you've been unconsciously holding and prompting you to let go. Essentially, PMR is a natural muscle relaxant.

PMR is not an ancient practice – it was developed by an American doctor, Edmund Jacobson, in the 1920s. Jacobson is known in the therapeutic community as "the man who invented relaxation", but no one can invent relaxation; humans are always rediscovering the natural state of peace and how to train the mind and body to get there more efficiently. Jacobson came up with the technique rather as a way to help his patients deal with anxiety and to sleep better.

INNER LABORATORY

Quick progressive muscle relaxation (PMR)

Try this very quick experiment, right now, to see how the PMR technique works. You can do this any time you need a moment to relax, not only when ready to sleep.

1. As you sit, inhale and squeeze your shoulders towards your ears. Even squeeze your facial muscles, puckering up your features to make a sour face.
2. With a big exhale, release your shoulders and allow your jaw to drop.
3. Take several deep breaths and notice if the whole area feels more relaxed than before.

DEEP SLEEP MEDITATION

Before bed, practise this whole-body progressive muscle relaxation (PMR) technique for deep relaxation. You can have a loved one read these steps to you, or you can read through them now and, when you try it at sleep time, remember that it is head to toe. You might miss out a few elements at first, but that won't matter too much. Then, guide yourself through it at night as part of your wind-down routine.

1. Lie on your back as symmetrically as possible. Open your arms and hands, as shown opposite.

2. Notice your whole body. Take several slow, conscious breaths and mentally set an intention to let go of the day. Tomorrow is a new day and you will awaken feeling rested and energized. Use this moment to acknowledge what you are grateful for.

3. Notice the sensations around your head. Inhale and squeeze your facial muscles, making a sour expression. Exhale to release and feel your facial muscles drop, especially your jaw.

4. Notice your shoulders. Inhale to squeeze your shoulders up towards your ears. And exhale to release. Bring your shoulder blades down away from your ears.

5. Bring your attention to your arms. Squeeze your hands into fists, bend your elbows, and lift your arms slightly. Exhale to release, allowing your arms to drop and your fingers to relax.

6. Feel your abdomen moving with your breath. Inhale to suck your navel in towards your spine. Squeeze for a moment and release.

7. Notice your hips, thighs, and gluteals. Squeeze your buttocks together to feel a lifting action. And exhale to release.

8. Notice your lower legs and feet. Gently curl your toes and point your feet. And release.

9. Now, once again, notice your whole body lying here. Squeeze everything at once. Your face, shoulders, arms, abdomen, buttocks, and feet. And release. Exhale to sigh it out. Feel your whole body drop.

10. Notice your breath, feeling a profound sense of release with each exhale. Consider counting your breath. Rather than counting sheep, count your breath backwards from 100 to 1.

Inhale, exhale: 100
Inhale, exhale: 99
Inhale, exhale: 98...

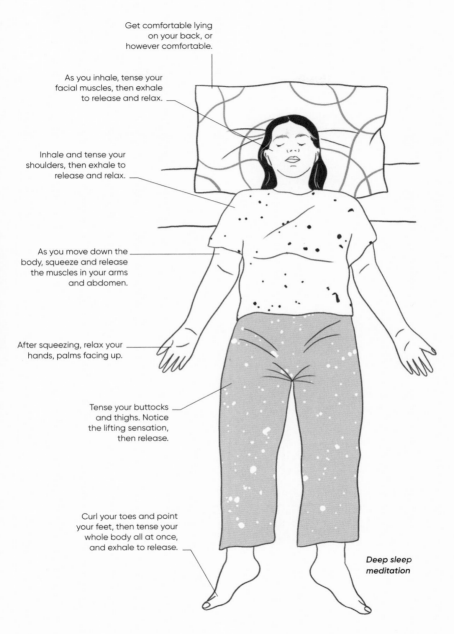

Get comfortable lying on your back, or however comfortable.

As you inhale, tense your facial muscles, then exhale to release and relax.

Inhale and tense your shoulders, then exhale to release and relax.

As you move down the body, squeeze and release the muscles in your arms and abdomen.

After squeezing, relax your hands, palms facing up.

Tense your buttocks and thighs. Notice the lifting sensation, then release.

Curl your toes and point your feet, then tense your whole body all at once, and exhale to release.

Deep sleep meditation

Reset your biological clock

Being more in tune with the hours of light and darkness can help you sleep at night and re-energize you during the day. Strategically integrating meditations, even short ones, into your day can optimize your internal biological clock.

Busy lives spent inside buildings, with artificial light, working late, or doing night shifts can mess with your natural sleep patterns. Your 24-hour cycles, called circadian rhythms, arise through multiple cues from your environment. For example, research shows that your retina takes in the colours of natural light to help you sync with the sun, setting your sleep–wake cycle. The blue hues of sunrise wake you up, the brightness of the midday sun peaks your energy, and the warm tones of sunset encourage release of the melatonin hormone, which promotes sleep. Ideally, get outside for at least 10 minutes during each of these times of day. Sitting near a window helps, but glass blocks some of the spectra of light.

MIDNIGHT MEDITATION

If you wake in the night, create a midnight oasis to help you drift back to sleep. Instead of looking at the clock, close your eyes and tune inwards to wind down.

1. Lie down: Reposition yourself and do any movements to get 5–10 per cent more comfortable.

2. Breathe down: Slow down your breathing. Bring most of the movement of your breath down to your abdomen. With each exhale, allow your muscles to release down. This will also decelerate your heart rate, promoting sleep.

3. Scan down: Slowly bring your attention through your body parts from head to toe, feeling a wave of relaxation travelling down your body.

4. Slow your thoughts down: When you get involved in a thought, remind yourself that you can address it better tomorrow with quality sleep behind you.

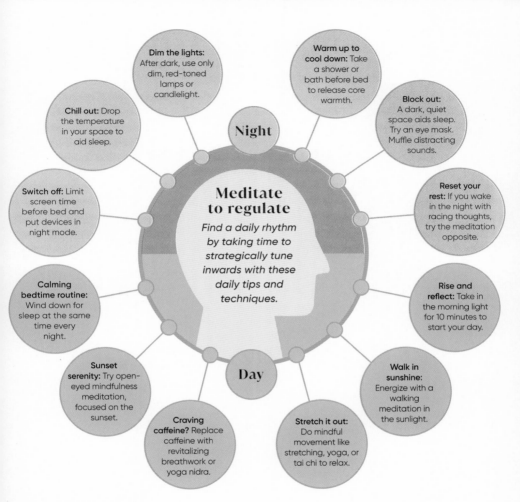

Night

Dim the lights: After dark, use only dim, red-toned lamps or candlelight.

Warm up to cool down: Take a shower or bath before bed to release core warmth.

Block out: A dark, quiet space aids sleep. Try an eye mask. Muffle distracting sounds.

Chill out: Drop the temperature in your space to aid sleep.

Reset your rest: If you wake in the night with racing thoughts, try the meditation opposite.

Switch off: Limit screen time before bed and put devices in night mode.

Meditate to regulate

Find a daily rhythm by taking time to strategically tune inwards with these daily tips and techniques.

Rise and reflect: Take in the morning light for 10 minutes to start your day.

Calming bedtime routine: Wind down for sleep at the same time every night.

Sunset serenity: Try open-eyed mindfulness meditation, focused on the sunset.

Walk in sunshine: Energize with a walking meditation in the sunlight.

Day

Craving caffeine? Replace caffeine with revitalizing breathwork or yoga nidra.

Stretch it out: Do mindful movement like stretching, yoga, or tai chi to relax.

INNER LABORATORY

Night watch

When you have a particularly good or bad night's sleep, log things that may be contributing to it, such as caffeine, exercise, or meditation. Remember that one night of data is not enough on which to make a decision. Look at trends over time to build your most efficient routine. You can conduct your own research on your sleep patterns by using a sleep-tracking app on your smartwatch or phone.

Improving immunity

Meditation has been shown to improve immune function on both a molecular and a practical level. It does this in part by boosting the activity and function of antibodies – protective proteins that combat invaders such as viruses.

Inside your body, wars are being fought at the microscopic level as you sip your coffee and go through your day. Armies of white blood cells with intense names such as "natural killer cells" circulate through your blood and lymph, assembling in areas where they are needed most to fight invaders (pathogens) that might make you ill. Ironically, one way you can help your cells fight more effectively is by cultivating a sense of peace within.

Natural defences

Routine meditation practice, along with a healthy lifestyle, helps your body do what it does best: maintain balance amid constant change and challenges. Taking a tranquil walk through the forest, for example, has been shown to boost your army of natural killer cells (see page 153 on connecting with nature).

Specifically, practising compassion has been shown to improve key markers of immune function. Compassion is a central pillar in many contemplative traditions, and it's often defined as a wish for others to be free of suffering. Some research suggests that even a few minutes of feeling compassion can make a difference to the strength of your immune system – which suggests that we don't need to meditate for long to see impactful benefits to our immunity and health.

Enhance your immunity

One study asked participants to cultivate compassion by focusing attention on their own heart beating while visualizing loved ones smiling and at ease for just five minutes. This visualization led to lower heart rates, which is indicative of relaxation. Researchers also measured SIgA (secretory immunoglobulin A), which is an antibody in your immune system that captures pathogens. More SIgA generally means that your immune system is ready to protect you. Generating compassion significantly increased SIgA – by as much as 240 per cent in some participants. Just

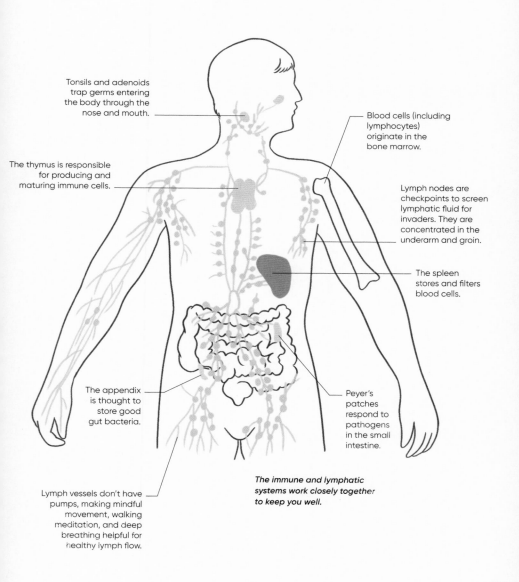

Tonsils and adenoids trap germs entering the body through the nose and mouth.

Blood cells (including lymphocytes) originate in the bone marrow.

The thymus is responsible for producing and maturing immune cells.

Lymph nodes are checkpoints to screen lymphatic fluid for invaders. They are concentrated in the underarm and groin.

The spleen stores and filters blood cells.

The appendix is thought to store good gut bacteria.

Peyer's patches respond to pathogens in the small intestine.

Lymph vessels don't have pumps, making mindful movement, walking meditation, and deep breathing helpful for healthy lymph flow.

The immune and lymphatic systems work closely together to keep you well.

five minutes of feeling connection and compassion led to antibody boosts lasting between one and six hours. Participants also reported an energy increase for the rest of the day. For more on the power of compassion for your mental wellbeing, see page 78.

Meditate for fewer sick days

A 2018 randomized controlled trial in the US with 413 participants compared a group who practised mindfulness-based stress reduction (MBSR – see page 16) to a group who exercised and an inactive control group to see who would most likely contract a respiratory infection, such as from the common cold or flu. Exercise is known to enhance immunity, making it a strong comparison group.

The results showed fewer missed work days due to respiratory infection in the mindfulness group (73) compared to the exercise group (82) and the control group (105). Other research supports the findings that both meditation and exercise reduce sick days and support immune function.

COMPASSIONATE HEART MEDITATION

Five minutes spent cultivating compassion is all you need to show measurable physiological changes for the better in immune function and stress resilience. Set a timer and try it for yourself!

1. Focus on the area around your physical heart as you breathe. You can place your hands on your heart or just mentally shift your consciousness to the area.

2. Envision someone you care about. Visualize them smiling. Imagine them happy and at ease.

3. As you breathe, alternate between focusing on your heart area and imagining your loved one being at ease.

4. Simply continue to do this for about five minutes.

When you feel ill

Did you know that meditation can help you feel better when you're ill? It can't magic away all illness, of course, but it can help you manage your symptoms.

Meditation has been shown to reduce inflammation and the likelihood of getting seasonal ailments in the first place. When you do get sick, it can bring some ease during recovery. Research shows that meditation and mindfulness-based practices measurably reduce not only stress hormones, but also key inflammatory markers in your blood, thereby helping your body and immune system to function optimally. (If you are experiencing digestive upset, turn to page 116.)

ONE-MINUTE MEDITATION
Time for medication

Before taking any prescriptions or medications, pause for a mindful moment. First, make sure you are taking what you need in the correct dosage. After taking the medications, close your eyes, take several full breaths, and visualize them supporting your body's healing and optimal function.

Your blood and lymph transport white blood cells through your body to attack invaders like viruses and bacteria. Drinking plenty of water encourages fluid flow so your cells can efficiently fight illness and release waste. Even when sick in bed, you can further enhance circulation with gentle ankle pump exercises by pointing your toes down and then flexing them up, taking deep breaths as you do so.

Prone position for better breathing

Lying on your belly, also called the prone position, can help improve distressed breathing, as with COVID-19 or other respiratory illness. Being face down relieves pressure on the lungs by taking off the weight of other organs and tissues, such as the heart, stomach, and breasts. For some, the position improves heart function and drains stuffed-up sinuses, too, making full breaths easier to take.

HEALING VISUALIZATION

Lie on your abdomen with your head to the side or face down, with your hands or pillows supporting your forehead so you can breathe well. Breathe through your nose (unless you are stuffed up). Guide yourself through these prompts or listen to a longer version at meditationfortherealworld.com/healing.

1. Deepen your breath, allowing your ribcage and lower back to expand three-dimensionally with the inhales, and release down and inwards with the exhales as much as is comfortably possible. Feel the movement of the back and sides of your ribcage as you recruit your diaphragm to take fuller breaths.

2. Once breathing like this becomes comfortable, for several deep breaths envision inhaling healing energy, then exhaling the waste from your body as it fights off illness.

3. Imagine your future self feeling better and doing the activities you love, reminding yourself that this will pass. Soon will be the time for such activities; now is the time for rest.

4. Relax for a while, anchoring your attention on internal flowing sensations. Feel the flow of fluids and breath as your body heals and rejuvenates.

Getting medical treatment

Whether you are undergoing a dental procedure or surgery in the hospital, mindfulness and meditation can help you get through it, especially if you feel anxious.

Before the treatment, meditation can ease your mind and lower levels of stress hormones. During procedures, visualization can help distract us, and after, it can support healing. Remember to always follow any instructions from your medical team, for example if there is a specific position for you to recover in, depending on the procedure.

Meditation can help calm and ground you before, during, and after treatment.

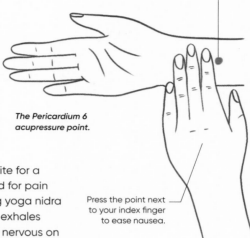

To find your P6 acupressure point, place your first three fingers on your wristline.

The Pericardium 6 acupressure point.

Press the point next to your index finger to ease nausea.

Look at the page opposite for a healing visualization, and for pain relief, consider practising yoga nidra (page 170) or elongated exhales (page 51). And if you feel nervous on the day, try to arrive early and, while in the waiting room, do a mini meditation to ground yourself.

Healing acupressure technique

Acupressure on the Pericardium 6 (P6) point on the wrist has been shown to ease nausea, including after an operation. To find this point, place your first three fingers below the prominent line of your inner wrist. The point located directly next to your index finger is where you will press with your thumb or any finger. As you press, imagine drawing tiny circles and take slow breaths with elongated exhales (see page 51). Massage this point as needed for three-minute sessions while sitting tall and breathing slowly.

ONE-MINUTE MEDITATION
Feeling safe and grounded

Feel the surfaces your body is touching, such as your feet on the floor, your body on whatever you are sitting or lying on. With each exhale, feel yourself releasing down into that surface. Visualize your muscles softening and your bones dropping down with each and every exhale.

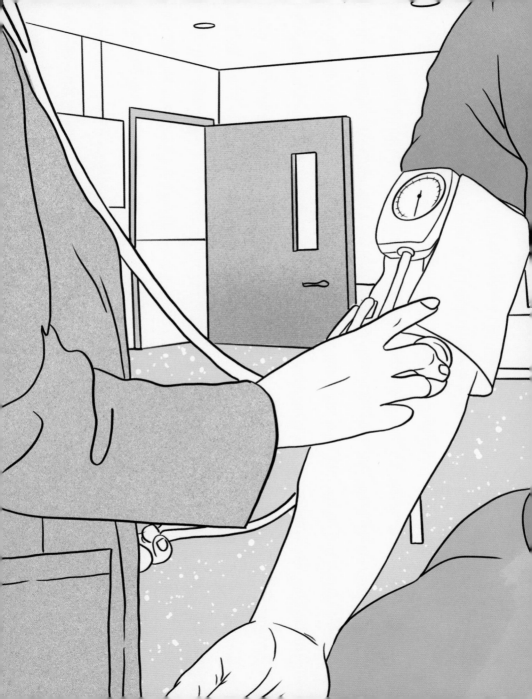

Relax to ease blood pressure

If you have high blood pressure, you are not alone. Try breathing and meditation techniques to help you relax and relieve the pressure both in the moment and the long term.

Over 30 per cent of adults worldwide have high blood pressure – defined as having a reading of over 140/90. Unfortunately, only one in five has it under control. Meditation can lower your blood pressure immediately if you are ever having a spike, but also, long-term practice could bring your blood pressure down by clinically meaningful levels.

Relaxation response

Cardiologist Dr Herbert Benson coined the term "relaxation response". Starting in the 1970s, he published research on this technique and mind-body medicine at Harvard Medical School and Massachusetts General Hospital. It refers to your ability to consciously encourage your body to release chemicals and brain signals to lower your blood pressure, decrease your resting heart rate, and put you in a deep state of relaxation. In this state, the parasympathetic nervous system (see page 50) takes over.

However, in our hectic, busy world, with days full of traffic jams and deadlines, many things can trigger the stress response when the sympathetic nervous system takes over. You can use the technique below anytime you feel your blood pressure rising, or you can use it as a simple daily practice.

INDUCING THE RELAXATION RESPONSE

This simple meditation is great for beginners. You can induce the relaxation response in yourself in just a few simple steps.

1. Sit in a comfortable position, in a chair or any way you want.

2. Close your eyes and relax consciously from head to toe.

3. Notice your breath as you breathe through your nose.

4. As you breathe out, repeat the word "one" to yourself silently.

5. Repeat this for 10–20 minutes. As thoughts come up, redirect yourself to your breath and the word "one".

White coat syndrome

White coat syndrome is a real phenomenon where people get higher blood pressure readings in the doctor's office due to anxiety. If this happens to you while getting your blood pressure taken, here is a technique you can try:

- Uncross your legs and sit tall.
- Breathe slowly, elongating your exhales to approximately twice the length of your inhales to ease stress (see page 51).
- If comfortable, breathe through your nose, or if you prefer you can inhale through your nose and exhale slowly through your mouth.

If you have 10 minutes in the waiting room, you can also use the relaxation response.

Good vibrations

Another method that is highly effective for lowering blood pressure may be a bit loud for the doctor's office, but it's great for when you are at home or in the car. Basically, it's humming – a bit like a bee!

Bee breath (bhramari pranayama) is a yoga breathing technique that has been shown to immediately decrease blood pressure, heart rate, stress markers, and anxiety levels. It has also been shown to release nitric oxide, which causes your blood vessels to relax and open (vasodilation), relieving the pressure.

Scientists believe that the acoustic vibration from humming has significant effects, including activation of the parasympathetic nervous system. The vibration of the head, sinus cavities, and trachea, and the elongated exhales, bring awareness to the area and influence your vagus nerve (specifically the ventral vagus), which helps you feel safe and calm.

INNER LABORATORY
Under pressure

If you have a blood-pressure cuff at home, do a little experiment. Take your blood pressure reading, then practise 10 minutes of the relaxation response (and/or the bee breath exercise) and then take your blood pressure again. See if the meditation has made a difference.

BEE BREATH

If you have a moment to yourself before a stressful incident that is causing your blood pressure to spike, practise this humming technique and let the vibrations do the rest.

1. Place your hands in your lap and close your eyes or gently cover your ears, eyes, and sinus cavities with your fingers to bring your attention inward to the vibrations.

2. Take a deep breath in through your nose, and on the exhale, hum quietly for as long as you comfortably can. Repeat for several rounds or until you feel relaxed.

Scientists believe that the acoustic vibration from humming has significant effects.

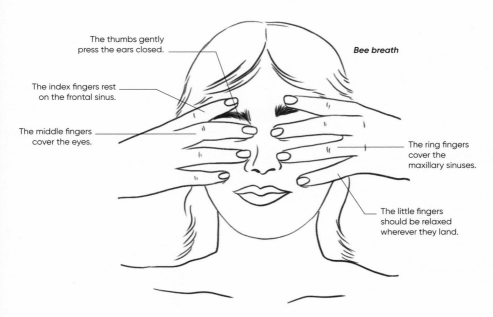

The thumbs gently press the ears closed.

Bee breath

The index fingers rest on the frontal sinus.

The middle fingers cover the eyes.

The ring fingers cover the maxillary sinuses.

The little fingers should be relaxed wherever they land.

Mindful eating

There is no doubt that food plays a crucial role in creating your healthiest self. You are what you eat, after all. Mealtimes are also integral in human bonding. Incorporating gratitude and mindfulness into mealtimes is a seamless way to fit meditation into your life – because everybody's got to eat.

Eating can be a joyous, sensory way of bringing mindfulness into your daily life, connecting you with your bodily sensations and with other people. Even temporarily refraining from eating can enhance your meditation and present-moment awareness. Fasting, often practised alongside meditation for spiritual or religious reasons, can improve alertness and mood, along with other health benefits, but consult with your healthcare provider to see if it's right for you.

Sensory cooking

Many people use cooking as a mindful relaxation practice. The colours, aromas, sizzling sounds, textures, and inevitable tastings provide an immersive multi-sensory experience that naturally keeps you present. Next time you are cooking, notice all five senses to infuse mindfulness into this creative act.

Gratitude before a meal

Blessings and gratitude are common practices before meals. When you sit down to eat, try affirming something you are grateful for. Take a mindful moment to recognize all the people and resources that contributed to bringing this food to you. When eating with others, say out loud, "I am grateful for this nourishing food," or, "I am so grateful to be sharing this food with you."

Post-meal mindful movement

After meals, go for a walk or do 10–15 minutes of light-to-moderate movement, such as a brief yoga video. Research shows that this lowers blood glucose spikes (and subsequent sugar crashes) by allowing your muscles to use the glucose for immediate energy.

INNER LABORATORY
Test your levels

Continuous blood glucose monitors (CGMs) are rising in popularity, not only for diabetics, but for people seeking optimal health and longevity. If you have a CGM, test the effects of the post-meal mindful movement. Alongside this, regular meditation practice has been shown to boost insulin sensitivity and lower fasting glucose levels.

THE RAISIN MINDFULNESS EXPERIMENT

Mindfulness-based stress reduction (MBSR), created by researcher Jon Kabat-Zinn, incorporates the classic raisin mindfulness experiment. This teaches us to recruit our senses into present-moment awareness and snap out of autopilot when we do everyday activities like eating. You can replicate this at home with a raisin or any small bite, including a grape, walnut, or piece of chocolate.

1. Start by holding the food. Rub it with your fingers and notice the texture, temperature, and weight.

2. Look at it and observe what you see – size, colour, texture, and anything else.

3. Smell it. Notice any effects; for example, you might be salivating in preparation. Even notice your feelings about it.

4. Place it on your tongue and feel it in your mouth.

5. Slowly chew, becoming aware of the taste and all your senses awakening. Chew many more times than you normally would.

6. Swallow slowly and notice how you feel.

Digestive health

Digestion is key to our wellbeing. It affects our energy levels, our mood, our physical health, even our skin. But the stresses of modern life can wreak havoc on our digestion, leading to chronic gut issues. The power to combat this can lie in food choices, and it can also lie in the mind.

There is now plentiful research that shows a strong link between the wellbeing of your brain and your "gut-brain" (the enteric nervous system). The vagus nerve connects these two systems. Feeling safe in meditation improves your vagal tone (which is associated with wellbeing). By reducing the burden of stress, meditation has been shown to support a healthy gut-brain and microbiome, promoting both a good mood and smooth digestion. When dealing with digestive issues, there are two factors to consider. First, establish a proper diet and determine food sensitivities, preferably with a qualified nutritionist. Be mindful of food triggers that may lead to digestive upset, joint pain, irritability, headaches, or migraines. Mindfulness helps us connect the relationship between our food choices and how we feel. The second major factor is stress. Your stress levels are likely correlated to your symptoms, especially with

MEDITATION TIPS FOR...

IBS/IBD

Meditation is well known to ease stress and inflammation. Allow your abdomen to move with your breath, as you may be holding tension in that area.

DIARRHOEA

Consider meditating in a warm bath to ease cramps. Stay hydrated and replenish with simple foods eaten slowly and mindfully. Elongated exhales help with cramping (see page 51).

CONSTIPATION/GAS/BLOATING

For constipation, drink plenty of water. Try a walking meditation (see page 144) to get your body moving effectively. Also try the mindful self-massage technique opposite.

concerns such as irritable bowel syndrome (IBS), which can cause abdominal pain, gas, bloating, diarrhoea, and/or constipation, and inflammatory bowel disease (IBD), which is marked by inflammation.

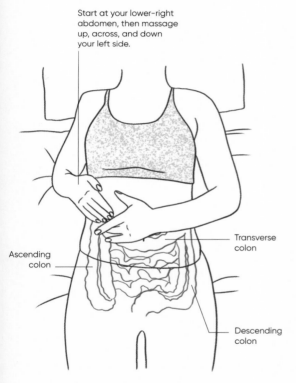

Start at your lower-right abdomen, then massage up, across, and down your left side.

Transverse colon

Ascending colon

Descending colon

Mindful abdominal massage can encourage gut movement.

MINDFUL ABDOMINAL SELF-MASSAGE

If you are constipated or bloated, try this massage to encourage movement in the gut (peristalsis) or release trapped gas. (If pregnant, please talk to your doctor first.)

1. Lying (or sitting) down, bring your right hand to your lower-right abdomen, directly above and inward from your hip point.

2. Massage up towards your ribcage over your ascending colon. With moderate pressure that doesn't increase pain, stroke with a gentle jostle in this direction.

3. Then massage over your transverse colon (from your right to your left).

4. Finally, massage down your descending colon on your left side.

5. Lift your hand and repeat this clockwise motion for up to five minutes. If there are any areas where you feel hardness, focus on that area to break up the foodstuff.

6. Afterwards, try a post-massage meditation by elongating your exhales for several minutes and feeling the physical results.

7. If needed, do some mindful movement or a walking meditation (see page 144) to encourage flow.

For PMS and cramps

Period troubles? You aren't alone. Many people have to deal with pre-menstrual syndrome (PMS), but the good news is that meditation and mindfulness practices have been shown to reduce symptoms, especially for severe cases.

PMS can include many symptoms such as bloating, mood swings, insomnia, painful cramping, and difficulty concentrating. A study conducted by Harvard researcher Dr Benson suggests that meditation works even better at alleviating these than other relaxing activities, such as chilling out with a good book. Practising yoga that incorporates poses, breathwork, and meditation has been shown to provide relief, too.

THE MENSTRUAL CYCLE

During the phases of the menstrual cycle, the body and mind go through changes and have different needs. Tailor your meditation practice to your personal cycle to optimize the benefits.

Menstruation

Days 1–5

A time of quiet reflection as the uterine lining sheds. Can cause cramping.

Try: yoga nidra (page 170) and bed yoga (opposite) with elongated exhales during cramps (page 51).

Follicular Phase

Days 6–13

A time of increased energy and drive as the ovary follicles mature.

Try: dynamic yoga (page 167), walking meditation (page 144), and mindful gardening (page 156).

Days 14–22

Marked by the egg's release and increased fertility. A time of peak energy and vibrancy.

Try: loving-kindness (page 79) and meditating with others (page 94).

Ovulation

Days 23–28

The body prepares for potential pregnancy or the next cycle. Can bring PMS.

Try: gratitude journalling (page 87) and bed yoga (opposite).

Luteal Phase

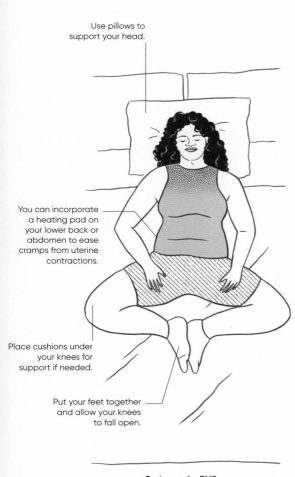

Use pillows to support your head.

You can incorporate a heating pad on your lower back or abdomen to ease cramps from uterine contractions.

Place cushions under your knees for support if needed.

Put your feet together and allow your knees to fall open.

Bed yoga for PMS and cramps.

BED YOGA

To deal with PMS and cramping, honour your body's request to slow and down and try this restorative bed yoga.

1. Lie on the bed with your feet together and knees falling open in a butterfly position. Place cushions under your knees if this is more comfortable.

2. Breathe low and slow, allowing your ribs and abdomen to move with your breath. If you are experiencing a wave of pain, inhale through the nose and exhale through the mouth slowly, elongating your exhales to about twice as long as the inhales. Keep your awareness resting on your breath. Stay in this position for 5–10 minutes.

3. If you like, try other positions and see how that feels for your body. For example, try lying on each side in a foetal position with a pillow between your knees, legs resting up against the wall or headboard, or a gentle twist with the pillow between your knees.

Meditation for pregnancy

Meditation can help you to relax and recharge during pregnancy, and to prepare for the birth.

Pregnancy is a life-changing experience, and hopefully one full of joy and excitement. It can also be a hectic and difficult time, however, as you prepare for your new arrival. Tiredness, anticipation, physical discomfort and, as you reach full-term, shallower breathing can all leave expectant mums feeling in need of a boost.

Meditative practices, such as breathing exercises and affirmations, have been shown to promote optimism and emotional stability amid the challenges pregnancy can present, helping you feel confident and prepared. If you are experiencing any anxiety at this time, meditation can also help alleviate these feelings. Learning to focus on moment-to-moment sensations builds trust in the body and reduces worry.

Pregnancy can be a time of introspection, and meditation can help you get to know yourself better, so you are well prepared when you meet new parts of yourself during labour and as a parent.

AFFIRMATIONS FOR PREGNANCY AND BIRTH

If you ever feel like you need encouragement during your pregnancy, try an affirmation. Read through these and notice if any feel right to you (or make up your own). Say this to yourself anytime you need it, during pregnancy or birth. Repeat it for several minutes to turn it into a personalized mantra meditation.

"I can do this."

"I trust myself."

"I trust my birth team."

"I trust my partner."

"I can make the best decisions for my baby and my body."

"I am present."

"I am surrounded by support and love."

"My body knows what to do."

"I can, I will."

DEEP RELAXATION MEDITATION

Try this meditation to encourage deeper diaphragmatic breathing, to help increase oxygen intake and aid relaxation.

1. Inhale deeply, feeling your lungs inflate. Your diaphragm engages downwards, massaging your internal organs and baby.

2. Exhale fully, feeling your lungs deflate. Your diaphragm relaxes back upwards, relieving pressure in the abdominal and pelvic cavities.

3. Continue breathing like this for several breaths, visualizing your diaphragm.

4. Next, with each inhale, envision and feel your pelvic floor relaxing downwards as you fill with oxygen.

5. With each exhale, envision and feel your pelvic floor slightly engaging upwards, mimicking the upward movement of your diaphragm as you empty your lungs.

ONE-MINUTE MEDITATION

Breaths of nourishment for your baby

Inhale, sending nourishment to your baby. **Exhale,** focusing on connecting your baby to the outside world, where they will soon be welcomed.

Breathe deeply and notice how the diaphragm and pelvic floor mimic each other in motion.

Engage the diaphragm as you breathe to massage your organs and baby.

Subtly allow the pelvic floor to engage then release to prepare for birthing.

As you approach full-term, you might experience shallower breaths, due to the changes in volume and pressure in the abdominopelvic cavity.

Easing perimenopause and menopause

Menopause is marked by menstruation stopping for a full year. The transition into it (perimenopause) can last for years, with symptoms such as low mood, anxiety, and sleep issues. Meditation helps bring inner stability amid hormonal chaos.

The hormonal changes that come with the perimenopause and menopause – which generally start in the mid- to late forties – especially the drastic fluctuation in oestrogen, can result in a rollercoaster of emotions and mental health struggles. Mindfulness meditation and mindful movement practices, including yoga, have been shown to help regulate mood, reduce depression symptoms, and improve sleep during this transition.

Mindfulness has been shown to help regulate mood and improve sleep during this transition.

Hot flushes and night sweats

Vasomotor symptoms such as body-heat changes can last for years during or after menopause. You might notice this as a sudden flare of heat rising through the chest, neck, and face, which can be accompanied by sweating and redness. Reduce the frequency by being mindful of your triggers: common triggers include caffeine, alcohol, spicy foods, restrictive clothing, and stress. Any meditation techniques you can do to reduce your stress will be beneficial, but in the heat of the moment, you can get immediate relief by changing how you breathe. A breathing technique that incorporates mouth breathing (see opposite) can help if you have a hot flush, as it takes advantage of the cooling effect of your saliva.

COOLING BREATH
(SITALI PRANAYAMA)

Try this cooling breath technique if you are feeling hot or stressed.

1. When ready, close your eyes and imagine you are in a cold environment, like walking through a beautiful snowfall or taking a dip in a refreshing lake.

2. Now roll your tongue and take a long inhale through your mouth as if you are sucking on a straw.

3. Close your mouth to exhale through the nose.

4. Repeat for several breaths until you feel calmer and any hotness has passed.

Combat the symptoms

There are many meditations you can try to help alleviate your specific symptoms. These include practices:
– to improve sleep (see page 100)
– to manage stress (see page 51), anxiety (see page 59), and depression (see page 55)
– to fight fatigue (see page 75)
– to improve concentration (see page 66)
– to ease headaches (see page 130) and body pain (see page 124)
– to feel more balanced; try alternate nostril breathing (see page 68)

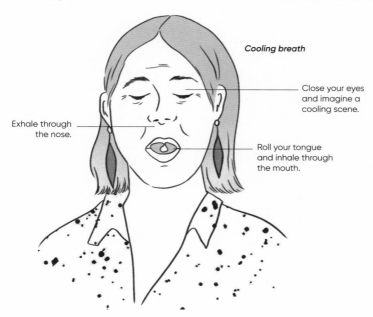

Cooling breath

Close your eyes and imagine a cooling scene.

Exhale through the nose.

Roll your tongue and inhale through the mouth.

Everyday pain relief

Back pain, aching joints, and other types of chronic pain can impact your everyday life and hold you back from activities you love, but it doesn't have to be that way.

Pain is complex. It can be a minor annoyance if you feel stiff from a day at your desk, or from tech neck, or it can be more persistent. Meditation has a natural analgesic effect. One 2021 study showed that mindfulness reduced optional opioid consumption in veterans with chronic pain. This result is hypothesized to be in part due to an increased ability to effectively regulate behaviours, as well as improving pain tolerance. All meditation can be helpful for pain over time, but you'll need to experiment to find the technique that works best for you.

Your alarm system

Your nervous system has an alarm system to protect you from threats. If you sense the building burning, your alarm sounds, telling you to get out. Likewise, if you burnt your hand on the stove, you would pull away. Short-lived pain from a possible injury is acute pain, but when pain becomes chronic – persisting for longer than three to six months – it behaves differently.

With chronic pain, as with trauma and anxiety, there is a faulty alarm system that may go off when a metaphorical candle is lit. This can happen when you gently bump your arthritic knee or you feel the early signs of a headache and your mind envisions how it might ruin your day. With time, we can be sensitized to pain, so that lesser stimulation hurts more. Your nervous system learns persistent pain, but the good news is that it can also unlearn this pain. Meditation can play a significant role in pain relief by helping to reprogram that faulty alarm.

A natural alternative to painkillers

Many painkillers have been shown to have negative and unintended side effects with long-term use, from addiction to organ damage. Interestingly, some over-the-counter pain pills have been shown not only to subdue physical pain, but also to dull emotions. As well as dampening knee pain or headaches, they seem to act as social analgesics, reducing empathy for others. In contrast, meditation boosts compassion and connection with others, while improving pain tolerance. While sometimes painkillers may be needed, meditation provides another option for the long term that helps you stay connected. It teaches us to be present with all feelings, even painful ones. Through acknowledgement of what is – rather than trying to resist it – suffering is eased. And you may then notice yourself reaching for optional pain pills less often.

Scan through the body, from head to toe.

Notice what sensations you feel beyond just "pain".

Recognize when areas of your body feel good or OK.

A body scan meditation can help you check in with how you're feeling.

ONE-MINUTE MEDITATION
A quick body scan

Check in with your body. What do you feel? Where do you feel it? Name it beyond the word "pain" (consider descriptive words like warm, tingly, tight, vibrating, pulsating, red...). Is there anything you can do to ease 5–10 per cent of that pain? Is your body asking for some sort of self-care or movement? (Explore your inner sensations further with a yoga nidra, on page 170.)

Meditation has a natural analgesic effect on us.

Pain flares

The nature of chronic pain is that it tends to flare. Mindfulness can help you notice triggers and early signs of flares so you can start self-care straight away. It's in the nature of your mind to skip forward to potential future pain and worry about how it might affect you or to lament any life-limiting pain you've experienced in the past. Sometimes, the brain can't tell the difference between real and imagined or remembered events – a similar cocktail of hormones and neurotransmitters is released regardless. So when your mind catastrophizes about a potential pain flare, it may exacerbate it by doing so. Meditation teaches us how to be more present with what is happening now and therefore to manage flares.

Feel it

Your body is constantly speaking to you, but unfortunately, chronic pain can lead to body disassociation, since trying to ignore and distract ourselves from the pain are common coping mechanisms. Your body starts by whispering requests, often for rest and relaxation. If you don't listen, the whispers turn into a loud voice and eventually a scream. Meditation helps you explore sensations with kindness and curiosity (rather than fear and dislike). Practising can improve body awareness, which can help you listen better to the messages your body is sending you while in the whisper stage. Body scans (like the one opposite) and yoga nidra (see page 170) can help you explore these sensations.

ONE-MINUTE MEDITATION

Be mindful of words

Through your day, notice labels that you apply (verbally or mentally) to painful areas of your body, such as "my bad knee", and reframe it as something less disparaging, like "the knee that needs more love" or something more neutral like "my tender knee". In these moments, take a few slow breaths and imagine sending love, healing energy, and even gratitude to that body part for all it does for you.

SENSATIONAL SCAN

This body scan meditation can be done seated or lying down, quickly or slowly. Feel each cue physically as you read, or linger on each instruction by pausing and closing your eyes. Note if there is any area your attention gravitates towards and listen to whatever messages are there, even the whispers.

1. Feel the temperature and movement of the air where your bare skin is exposed. Feel the weight of the fabric on your skin in the areas you are clothed.

A little can make a big difference

Think you need to devote a long time to meditating to reduce your pain? One study conducted at Wake Forest University and published in the Journal of Neuroscience *showed that just four 20-minute mindfulness sessions dramatically decreased pain-related brain activity and reduced the unpleasantness of pain by 57 per cent and the pain intensity by 40 per cent.*

2. Feel your head, shoulders, elbows, wrists, and hands. Feel your spine, hips, knees, ankles, and feet.

3. Feel your whole body at once.

4. Feel the left side of your body, then the right.

5. Feel the front of your body, then the back.

6. Feel the shape and outline of your body. Then, observe sensations directly under your skin. Move deeper and feel the flow of fluids through your body. Perhaps you feel a pumping, a pulsation, a vibration... Notice all the movement present even though you are still.

7. Feel the boundary of your body blur so the outline becomes fuzzy. Imagine your energy fusing with the energy around you. What is it like to feel expansive and beyond the physical body? Rest in this awareness of being an energetic being for a few moments.

Relief for arthritis

Over 500 million people worldwide are living with osteoarthritis, and the chances of developing it only increase with age. A clever visualization technique, however, can offer real results.

If you live long enough, you will likely experience the natural wearing down of the joints that is osteoarthritis, most commonly in the hands, hips, and knees. With osteoarthritis, the space in the joints typically gets smaller as glass-like cartilage on the ends of the bones begins to wear down, eventually leading to bone-on-bone contact, but you can find relief with a meditative magic trick: visualization. Well, it's not magic; it's just a demonstration of the power of the mind on the body.

Visualizing flexibility and strength

Visualization is a powerful tool used by everyone from monks to Olympic athletes, because it works. That's right – simply imagining that you're stretching or engaging certain muscles has been shown to improve flexibility and strength (even without moving). This research shows the power of your mind. Does this mean that you should skip exercise and just lie in bed imagining you are at the gym? Of course not! However,

visualization can be helpful, especially during times of healing and recovery, or for beginners trying to exercise without increased pain. Mindfully move within your own comfort zone but visualize moving with a full range of motion.

HAND RELAXATION MEDITATION

In this visualization practice, you will focus on expanding that joint space in your wrist and hand. This can help to alleviate any discomfort and pain you might be experiencing.

1. Place your hands together, side by side, little fingers touching, and lining up the most prominent lines on your inner wrists.

2. Keeping these lines touching, turn your palms towards each other and notice if one hand has longer fingers than the other. If so, choose the hand with shorter fingers to focus on. If they are the same length, randomly choose one hand.

3. In your chosen hand, imagine space in the wrist between all the carpal bones. Take several breaths and visualize that space expanding.

4. Shift your attention to the palm and imagine the space in between the metacarpal bones expanding.

5. Imagine each finger lengthening one by one, from the palm to the fingertips. Take several breaths, imagining space in the finger joints.

6. Imagine the whole hand as spacious. Picture a soft lengthening from your wrist, through your hand, past your fingertips. You may notice a gentle twitch or pulsation. Look at your hand and notice what is happening. Does your hand look or feel different? Perhaps you can feel the flow of circulation and the buzz of awareness. Do you feel relief?

7. Realign the prominent lines of your wrists.

8. Turn your palms back towards each other and notice if the length has changed.

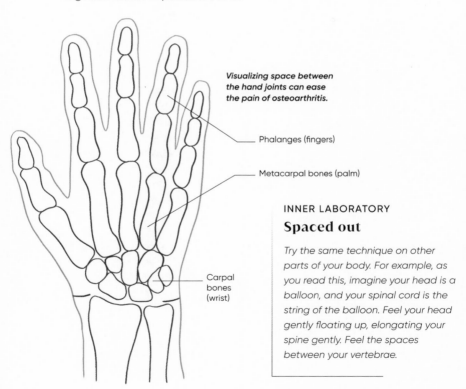

Visualizing space between the hand joints can ease the pain of osteoarthritis.

Phalanges (fingers)

Metacarpal bones (palm)

Carpal bones (wrist)

INNER LABORATORY
Spaced out

Try the same technique on other parts of your body. For example, as you read this, imagine your head is a balloon, and your spinal cord is the string of the balloon. Feel your head gently floating up, elongating your spine gently. Feel the spaces between your vertebrae.

Unravelling headaches

Research suggests that meditation can help reduce the frequency, intensity, and duration of headaches and migraines. Scientists believe it helps by reducing the stress burden and mitigating pain.

One fascinating trial published in *Behavioral Medicine* in 2017 found that adding a spiritual spin to meditation eased migraines best and led to participants taking fewer optional analgesics. Since spirituality is a personal practice, one participant chose to replace the word "God" with "Mother Earth". Personalizing the practice can get the best results. Mindfulness can help you recognize your unique triggers and early signs of a headache or migraine, so you can practise self-care early and possibly prevent a flare-up.

Triggers and signs of headache and migraine

Common triggers: *Disrupted sleep, stress, change of weather, bright or flickering lights, loud noises, dehydration, strong smells.*
Early signs: *Dull pain, irritability, specific food cravings, neck stiffness, increased urination, frequent yawning, pins and needles in a limb, an aura of light or colours.*

UNTANGLING TENSION

Removing yourself from your triggers, relaxing your body, and saying a mantra can be very effective in reducing headaches.

1. Find a comfortable place away from bright lights, annoying sounds, and anything else you think might have prompted your headache. Sit in a comfortable chair or lie down with pillows and blankets.

2. Do an upper-body scan and release. Start by gently moving your jaw and facial muscles to make silly faces. Allow your jaw to drop. Imagine your eyes sinking back. Let the worry lines on your forehead melt away.

3. Envisage a wave of relaxation down your scalp to your neck and shoulders.

4. Then, invite subtle movements into your neck and shoulders. Try looking over each shoulder, tilting your head, and rolling your shoulders a few times.

Find somewhere quiet, wear earplugs, or listen to nature sounds.

If you feel a headache coming, avoid triggers.

Get away from bright lights and blue lights (such as screens).

5. Imagine a knot inside your head being unravelled, little by little, with each exhale. Invite that feeling of satisfaction of a knot being loosened.

6. Repeat your chosen mantra. Choose a phrase that is comfortable for you and your beliefs, and say it alongside your inhale and exhale. For example:

INHALE: *"[God, any word for God, the universe, Mother Earth] is..."*
EXHALE: *"[love, peace, joy, good]."*

Repeat for several minutes to the rhythm of your breath.

Try a hot or cold compress

A heating pad can dilate blood vessels, relaxing the muscles on your scalp, neck, or shoulders. A cool, wet towel or ice pack to the head or neck constricts the blood vessels and has a numbing effect. Research shows both can be helpful for headaches, so experiment to find which works best for you.

CHAPTER 4

MEDITATION FOR EVERY DAY

We are all busy, with a long to-do list to manage. It can be hard to find time for friends and family – and even harder to take time for ourselves. However, even a one-minute meditation or a single mindful breath counts.

You don't need a quiet, serene setting like a yoga studio to have an effective meditation. In the following pages, you'll discover how the sounds around you, touch, and being in nature can enhance your practice. You don't need to be still, either. You can experience meditation in motion with yoga, tai chi, and dance.

The beauty of mindfulness is that it can be a part of your life 24/7. Discover how to harness its power while you're commuting, cleaning, gardening, walking to work, exercising, or even washing your face. Ultimately, it's not what you do but how you do it that matters. The calm you cultivate is contagious; it will affect others around you, enrich your relationships with them, and elevate your life.

Creating daily habits

Think you don't have time to meditate? Infuse mindfulness into everyday activities, such as while getting ready in the morning, packing your kid's lunch, or washing the dishes at the end of a long day.

If you're struggling to see how you can fit meditation into your busy life, start with micro-moments and then notice how mindfulness begins to pervade nearly everything you do. With practice, it becomes second nature. Your daily activities provide natural ways to experience the power of being present.

Skincare

Make your daily skincare a mindful ritual. Massage in moisturizers, sunscreens, or topical medication, imagining each is a nourishing elixir or invisible protective shield. Observe self-criticism, especially when facing the mirror. What's it like to look yourself in the eyes (rather than into your perceived flaws)?

Showering

Use your daily time in the shower to either recharge or relax. Instead of fighting mental arguments or time travelling in your head, simply be in the shower. This small choice can make a big difference. Be mindful as the water cascades over your skin and you massage in your shampoo.

ONE-MINUTE MEDITATION
Brushing teeth

Each time you brush your teeth, be mindful, rather than rushing to think about the next thing you need to do. Be fully present with the sensations and sounds. It might sound strange but this is a good technique for showing you how your mind can stay in the present.

Therapeutic housework

Transform housework into a moving meditation. Approach tasks as mindful exercise by being aware of your body movements: hinge from the hips and knees rather than rounding your back to bend over, widen your stance in squats, take breaks as needed, and respect your body's natural limitations. While cleaning, set an intention to clear mental clutter. Notice when your mind wanders and anchor yourself to the sensations of your body and breath while performing the task.

PHYSIOLOGICAL SIGH

You may notice that you sigh as you go about your day, but have you ever wondered why we sigh? It seems to be our body's way of regulating our breath and naturally releasing some emotional weight from anxiety, stress, or pain. Take a sigh as a cue to practise what Stanford neuroscientist Andrew Huberman calls "the physiological sigh". You can do this several times while doing any activity like washing the dishes.

1. Inhale fairly deeply through your nose. Then, inhale one last bit to expand your lungs.

2. Exhale as slowly and as fully as possible through your mouth, like an intentional sigh.

3. Repeat a few times, and notice afterwards if you feel more relaxed.

Connect with bodily sensations as you breathe to make each task mindful.

Be mindful of your posture while doing housework.

Daily activities offer a perfect way to bring mindfulness into your day.

Tune in to sound

It's a common idea that you need silence to meditate. In fact, music and sound can help you to relax. You can also meditate with any background noise – the sound of kids playing or street noise can even enhance your practice.

Traditionally, chanting and listening to sacred music have been incorporated into meditation practices, and now scientists are uncovering the mechanisms behind this sound wisdom. It seems that rhythmic vocal repetition is good for your heart. Italian cardiologist Luciano Bernardi found that "Om mani padme hum" – a traditional Tibetan chant – slowed respiration to six breaths per minute (bpm) (12–20 bpm is normal adult respiration). Bernardi also found that chanting enhanced heart-rate variability (HRV), i.e. having variant time between heartbeats. This is a good thing. Younger people and athletes tend to have high HRV. Chanting also improved the sensitivity of pressure receptors (baroreceptors) in the arteries. This means chanting can train your heart and blood vessels to respond better to whatever arises, making you resilient under stress.

Singing with others

Chanting "om" in yoga class, singing hymns in church, or even belting "Happy Birthday" at a party synchronizes autonomic rhythms in the group, helping you feel a deeper social bond. There is a reason cultures have traditional songs, countries have national anthems, and spiritual practices use songs to help people relax and feel connected. It works. So look for ways to bring these elements into your life more often – you might like to join a choir or simply sing at home.

OM (AUM)

"Om" has been used for meditation and yoga practice for millennia. It seems chanting "om" may have benefits over other sounds. One study in 2011 used fMRI scans to compare the sound with "sssss" and found that "om" deactivated many brain areas, notably the right amygdala, which is associated with fear.

*Different sound frequencies (or colours)
can aid your meditation practice.*

White noise

Whirring, humming, hissing: for sound masking, enhanced focus.

Pink noise

Rainfall, rustling leaves: for better sleep, improved memory.

Brown noise

Waterfalls, thunder: for relaxation, better sleep, enhanced focus.

Sound frequencies

Sound, like light, is made of waves, and the frequency of the waves affects how you perceive them. Just as white light is a combination of all the colours, white noise (such as a whirring fan or humming air conditioner) contains waves across all frequencies we can hear, helping to muffle other noises. Pink noise (such as rainfall) and brown noise (such as rumbling thunder), on the other hand, limit higher frequencies and have been shown to enhance memory consolidation and slow-wave deep sleep. Listening to any of these sounds, either in the real world or via recordings, can promote relaxation and focus during your meditation practice or even during everyday activities.

Binaural beats

Binaural beats consist of two tones of distinct frequencies, which are intentionally designed to be heard in each ear through headphones. When perceived by the brain as a unified tone, they may synchronize neural activity through a phenomenon called entrainment. This can alter the way you think and feel. Measured in hertz (Hz), specific frequencies of sound (like in binaural beats) have been shown to change brainwaves:

- **4–8 Hz** binaural beats have been shown to induce theta brainwaves, which are associated with a meditative state.
- **8–13 Hz** promotes alpha waves, which are also associated with a meditative state.
- **16–25 Hz** binaural beats induces beta brainwaves, which may boost concentration.
- **40 Hz** tones have been shown to induce gamma waves, which may improve working memory (see page 40 for a chart of the different types of brainwaves).

Music intensity

External rhythms influence internal rhythms. You embody acoustics viscerally, from the vibrations of singing bowls to the blast of music from your speakers in the car. Relaxing, slower-tempo music measurably slows the heart rate and respiratory rhythm, while varying tempos affect you similarly to a dynamic yoga practice, bringing more presence to the silence. After changing intensity, focus, and respiration through a song, the pauses and silence tend to evoke a deeper sense of calm.

Sound bathing

Sound baths are meditative experiences where sound vibrations through the whole body become the object of your attention. Try attending a sound bath or sound healing session, which is often held in conjunction with yoga or meditation classes. At these sessions highly resonant, immersive sounds are often made with metal or crystal singing bowls. You can also do sound bathing in natural surroundings, listening to rustling trees, waves on a beach, or the sound of a waterfall.

SOUND MEDITATION

Choose whatever sound appeals to you today – it could be relaxing music, recorded sounds that you find online, or you might go outside and find a place with appealing natural sounds, like waves, or rustling trees.

1. Sit comfortably, and read the steps. When ready, close your eyes and listen to your chosen sounds.

2. Notice any sounds that are present for a few moments.

3. Focus on sounds far away. Listen for the furthest sounds possible.

4. Now, focus on sounds nearby.

5. Now, listen to even closer sounds.

6. With all these sounds around you, try to bring the sound of your own breath to the foreground of your awareness.

7. Notice the rhythm of your breath. Does it sync with or mirror the sounds around you?

8. Now observe all the sounds, far away and up close, simultaneously.

9. Notice any emotions and visceral feelings attached to the sounds.

10. Note how the sounds arise, transform, and disappear naturally. They are transient, impermanent.

Focus on visuals

You can use any favourite object to meditate with, and to focus the mind. This can be a small item, such as a beautiful artwork, or think larger, to the sky. This not only concentrates your mind in the moment; it also helps you see the world afresh, often with wonder and amazement.

Any item can be a focus for meditation, from a small object on your desk to a mountain in the distance. In a yoga pose, you may look at your hands, and while meditating you may look towards the tip of your nose. You might like to sit gazing at a favourite object, such as a piece of art, a small sculpture, a hand-made item, a piece of writing, or a few flowers. Anything around you can be viewed with mindfulness.

The world around us

Many people think of space as nothing, yet they see an object such as a vase as something. However, the true worth of a vase is in the space it provides for filling, just as the essence of your home is not the walls but the spaces they create. In fact, what seems like a solid object is mostly made up of space between and within its atoms, and since you are made entirely of atoms too, the majority of you is space – and energy.

You are made of stardust. Astrophysicists estimate that nearly all the atoms in your body originated from stars. Through powerful explosions, stars became supernovas and spread cosmic dust filled with the elements that eventually created the Earth and human beings. So, how does this fit in with meditation? Try the one-minute meditation (below). You come from the stars that you can see. Stargazing can be a profound, contemplative experience, and can put our worries into perspective.

ONE-MINUTE MEDITATION
Mindful stargazing

Whenever possible, take a minute to look at the night sky. Notice the stars above you. Does one in particular catch your attention? Note the current phase of the moon. Is it waxing (getting fuller) or waning (approaching a new moon)? Breathe deeply to take it all in.

A scientific basis

Basking in lunar light (or moon bathing) may sound like mysticism, but it could enhance your mental health. Research illuminates the benefits of observing nocturnal nature, including positive emotions, greater connection with nature, personal growth, and even transcendent experiences. Allowing your eyes to acclimatize to the night sky – rather than the blue light of screens and artificial bulbs – also helps regulate your melatonin hormone levels and, thus, your sleep–wake cycle (see page 102).

Anything around you can be viewed with mindfulness.

SEEING THE WORLD WITH NEW EYES

Sit tall as you read this short meditation. Then, integrate this exercise into moments throughout your day to see things from a different perspective.

1. Start by looking at the words in the book in front of you. Then, see the background space that surrounds them.

2. Now, look around the room as you normally see it. Usually, we are focused on stuff, such as objects in cluttered rooms that need tidying. Instead, be like an artist and see the shapes and contours of the space around and between the object. Approach with curiosity and attention, as if you are about to paint the background space of a masterpiece.

3. Allow a soft gaze and let everything in at once. How does it feel to see the world in this spacious way?

The power of touch

Touch is our first sense to develop and is integral to lifelong emotional regulation. Physical sensation is always there and constantly changing, making it an excellent anchor to the present moment in meditation and when being mindful during your day.

As you are reading this, can you sense your skin? Skin is the largest organ in your body. As a physical barrier, it both protects you from and perceives the external world. Your sense of touch is responsible for the warm and fuzzy feelings we get from hugging a loved one, the electric touch of a budding romance, the creepy crawlies when we feel watched, the relief of pain from a body-scan meditation, and the goosebumps when we are touched by a sweet gesture or serendipitous moment. We use touch to connect to the outside world, but we can also use it to connect deeply to our inner world.

Internal body awareness

"Interoception" is our internal body awareness, which allows us to perceive ourselves. It includes our skin's ability to perceive our inner world, directly under the surface and deep within, such as feeling our heart pounding, our tummy grumbling, and even gut feelings or that sinking in our chest when something isn't right. Improved interoception may help you tap into intuition. And the more aware you are of your body's signals and requests, the more able you are to support what it needs.

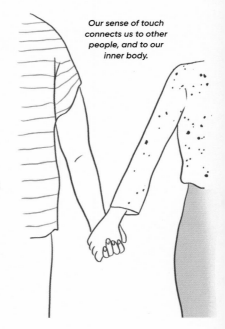

Our sense of touch connects us to other people, and to our inner body.

EXPLORE YOUR SENSE OF TOUCH

In this meditation, you are going to focus on your own sense of touch. This helps you to become more aware of your inner body, your "interoception". Sit, or lie comfortably.

1. First, feel the surface of your skin. Notice areas that are physically touching something. Can you feel the weight of your clothing? Notice areas that are not touching anything. Can you feel the flow and temperature of the air on your skin?

2. Now, feel the outer boundary of your entire body, bound by your skin. Can you feel the shape of it?

3. Bring your awareness a little deeper to right under your skin – an internal landscape of sensation and vibration.

4. Focus attention on the palms of your hands, which have an extraordinary number of nerve receptors. Feel your hands holding sensation, vibration – whatever you feel – for several moments.

5. Now, place your hands on your heart. Can you feel it beating – an automatic electrical and mechanical pump nourishing your body with oxygenated blood?

6. Place your hands on your knees. Feel free to lovingly massage them to ease any pain, stimulate circulation, and aid healing. Inhale, bringing gratitude to your knees for all the places they take you.

7. Exhale, and feel your feet on the ground or surface below. Feel your whole body bathed in sensation.

Walking meditation

Taking a walk can clear the mind between work emails. A walking meditation has even greater benefits, so let's look at how you can bring this practice into your everyday life.

Today, our lifestyles are more sedentary than ever, and it's spectacularly bad for our health – some say sitting is the new smoking. Walking has been shown to reduce anxiety and depressive symptoms, while improving balance and preventing falls. Doing a walking meditation is a practical, healthy habit to prevent and alleviate the harmful side effects of sitting for too long. Walking in general has numerous benefits, which include:

- improving blood and lymph flow and helping to prevent and alleviate foot and ankle swelling by pumping fluids back to your heart.
- improving postural awareness.
- alleviating the stress of sitting for long periods, and whatever you were doing while sitting.
- encouraging healthy digestion by getting your gut moving and helping to keep you regular.

Even a two-minute walk can make a difference. Adding meditation connects you to your surroundings and eases the mind.

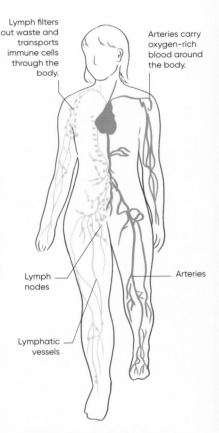

Lymph filters out waste and transports immune cells through the body.

Arteries carry oxygen-rich blood around the body.

Lymph nodes

Arteries

Lymphatic vessels

Walking improves lymph and blood flow around the body. The movement in the hips and swing of the arm especially help lymphatic flow.

MEDITATION ON THE MOVE

Your walk to work or to the shops is an opportunity to fit this kind of meditation practice (and the resulting peace of mind) into your busy day. And it's easy to learn, too.

1. Find a place to practise. This can be inside or outside, in a city or in nature. If your space is limited, you can pace in a straight line or in a circle (clockwise, as some traditions practice).

2. Notice the present moment. While standing, feel your feet on the ground. Become aware of your posture. Recruit all your senses to become aware of all aspects of the present moment. What do you see? Hear? Smell? Taste? Physically feel?

3. Walk mindfully with your breath. Notice your natural breathing rate. Find the rhythm of walking that flows easily with your breath. Count how many steps you naturally take on the inhale and how many you take on the exhale, which may be longer. Allow your lungs and body to choose the rhythm and simply notice. As you continue to walk or you walk uphill, you may notice that the rate changes.

4. Continue walking for as long as is comfortable. You could start with five minutes, or walk for longer – however much time you have. As you walk, consider using the following cues to bring your mind back to the present moment as it naturally wanders:

Touch the earth with love as if you are kissing it with your feet.

Imagine what it would feel like to walk as the happiest person on earth.

Remember, there is no need to hurry because there is no goal of a destination.

Allow each step to bring you back to the present moment.

Consider saying "yes" or "thank you" as your mantra with each step you take.

Smile softly. Allowing a gentle half-smile will bring calm and delight to the practice.

De-stress your commute

Commuting can be an act of getting from point A to point B on autopilot. As a result, it can feel like precious lost time and sometimes, when things don't go according to plan, it can be infuriating. Rather than being mindless, however, it can be an opportunity to be mindful.

While stuck in traffic, notice if you feel anxious, angry, or restless. When irritation takes hold, notice how the anger feels physically... what happens? Do you raise your shoulders and tense your jaw? Can you feel your blood pressure rising and your heart pounding? First, feel it in your body. Just by noticing, you may relax.

Then, notice how pointless it is to be agitated. Does it help? Is it worth the toll on your body and mental health? Sure, maybe a little frustration will lead to you leaving earlier for work the next day, but does playing things over and over in your head help? Listening to music can help you relax. Singing is even better! The elongated exhales, and even the vibrations, may influence your vagus nerve (see page 50), helping you to feel calm and connected. Alternatively, try three deep breaths or physiological sighs (see page 135) to allow the feelings to dissipate.

When frustration hits, take control of how you respond with mindfulness and calming breaths.

ONE-MINUTE MEDITATION
Wait with compassion

Another way to pass the time while waiting in traffic or for the next train is to send loving-kindness to a loved one or stranger you see by repeating kind words silently (and without staring, of course): *"May they be safe. May they be healthy. May they be joyful. May they be free from suffering. May they be at ease."*

TRAVEL MINDFULNESS

Make the most of your commuting time by using it to practise mindfulness. When you are mindful, you may notice that simple things become more interesting.

1. Take in your sensory experience.

2. Observe how everything changes around you with time. Notice the landscape or cityscape as you travel past, the patterns in bricks and tiles, the trees overhead.

3. Bring your breath to the foreground of your attention, while remaining acutely aware of your changing environment in the background.

At the airport and in flight

Some people love air travel, taking them to new places and to meet loved ones. For others, time in an airport is boring and stressful, and many deal with a fear of flying. Meditation can offer solace for all these travel experiences.

Longer waits, like in the airport, can provide an opportunity to practise a formal seated meditation. Plus, mindfulness while travelling can help you stay safe and attentive, while enjoying the journey.

WAITING AT THE AIRPORT

Before a flight, find somewhere comfortable to sit and try this meditation. It is very useful if you have a delay. Also, consider a walking meditation (see page 144) through the terminal.

1. While seated, keep your eyes open to remain alert. You may look out of the window at planes taking off. You could also observe the flow of people around you. Notice any judgements that may arise and let them go. Try to keep your gaze soft and neutral.

2. You may want to integrate sound – listen to calming music through headphones, or embrace the noises around you as objects of your attention to stay present. Alternatively, you can use earplugs to mask the noise, if you prefer.

3. Chances are you have been scurrying about to get here, so sit tall and notice how stillness feels.

4. For a few moments (or minutes) each, notice your five senses: sights, sounds, physical sensations, smells, and tastes.

5. Now, take in the full three-dimensionality of the present moment. Notice all your senses simultaneously. If you prefer, you can come back to any one sense that helped you feel at ease.

You can feel grounded even when in the air.

Fear of flying

Nervousness can escalate into a phobia when imagining worst-case scenarios. When you are on high alert, clear the skies of your mind by **orienting**, **moving**, and **grounding**. This "OMG" method was created by Steve Haines, author of *Anxiety Is Really Strange*, to find internal safety when feeling overwhelmed.

• **Orient:** Rather than a imagining the worst-case scenario, acknowledge what is happening right now. What can you see? Hear? Touch?

• **Move:** Even small ways of mobilizing can help you feel less out of body and more in control. Before a flight, try and move around, walking in the terminal. If you are on the plane, and space is tight, try the following:

    a. readjust your posture and feel the points of contact of your body on the chair.

    b. squeeze and release muscles like your thighs or fists.

    c. touch something with your hands, like your armrest, your lap, or your companion's hand.

    d. wiggle your toes.

• **Ground:** You can feel grounded even when in the air. Focus on:

    a. feeling your feet touching the floor below.

    b. feeling the movement of your breath in your abdomen.

    c. observing your body releasing down with each exhale.

    d. regulating your breath, as in the next technique.

CALM BREATHING

During take-off, landing, and times of turbulence, try this breathing technique. This can help regulate your respiration and blood pressure. Studies show that it is particularly beneficial to slow your breathing to 5–6 breaths per minute (bpm). Five seconds each for the inhale and exhale amounts to 6 bpm. The "and" in the exercise below may bring you to 5.5 bpm.

1. Inhale and exhale for slightly more than five seconds by saying to yourself:

"Inhale, 2, 3, 4, 5, and...

Exhale, 2, 3, 4, 5, and..."

2. Inhale through the nose and exhaling through the mouth with pursed lips for several breaths. Resume nose breathing with the count once you have settled.

3. Repeat for as long as you need. Make sure you are breathing fully into the belly and not just into the chest.

Feeling well on the flight

If you are experiencing nausea, headache, sweats or chills, or dizziness, try these tips and be mindful of what your body needs:

• *Increase the airflow around you by opening the vent above you fully.*

• *Yawn to equalize the air pressure in your inner ear.*

• *Regulate and slow your breathing, especially during turbulence, which can lead to breath-holding.*

• *Acupressure on the wrist can help with symptoms of nausea. (See page 109 to try this out.)*

• *Give your eyes a rest. Either close them or look out of the window and fix your gaze on the horizon.*

MINDFUL MOVEMENT

Sitting for long periods on a plane can make you feel sluggish and uncomfortable, so try this mindful movement that you can do in your seat. It can also help to prevent oedema (a build-up of fluid), especially in the feet and ankles, and other circulation issues, which are common during flights due to cabin pressure and being sedentary for too long.

1. Feel your feet on the floor. Lift your toes, then relax them down. Now lift your heels, then relax them down. Repeat around 30 times.

2. March your legs as if you are walking on the spot. Take 20 imaginary steps.

3. Lift your heels slightly off the floor and draw circles with your ankles – 10 in each direction.

4. Repeat this every hour or so.

5. If space, stretch your upper body, too. Even small movements that don't interfere with your neighbour make a difference.

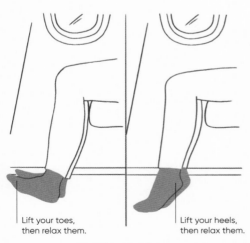

Lift your toes,
then relax them.

Lift your heels,
then relax them.

*Mindful exercises in your
seat can help circulation.*

Connecting with nature

Meditation has always been intimately connected to the natural world. The Buddha achieved the highest form of spiritual unity, also known as enlightenment or Nirvana, sitting near a river under a large fig tree called the Bodhi tree, or "tree of awakening".

Today, many of us recognize that taking breaks from the hustle and bustle of daily life to enjoy nature is essential for our overall wellbeing, and science is now illuminating the powerful effects it has on us, with a growing body of research supporting the benefits that spending time in nature has on our health – from reducing stress to facilitating healing. One study, published in the journal *Nature* in 2019, surveyed nearly 20,000 people and determined that spending at least two hours in nature weekly is associated with good health outcomes and wellbeing.

ONE-MINUTE MEDITATION
Ground down

Next time you have the opportunity, slip off your shoes and place your bare feet on the grass. Imagine you are inhaling energy as radiant light up from the earth. With each exhale, visualize energy settling down into the earth.

The power of green and blue

Even a glimpse of nature in your day can make a difference. If you can't make it to a forest or lake, simple acts like sitting near a fountain or taking your shoes off in a grassy patch have been shown to lead to meaningful health improvements. Here are just some of the ways these tranquil environments can benefit our minds and bodies, including in urban environments:

Green and blue spaces

Green spaces – such as public parks, roof gardens, or balconies – can have profound health-promoting effects, including boosting happiness. Blue spaces – such as the ocean or even a city fountain – have similar effects, with the added meditative rhythm of the movement of water to promote clear thinking and calm.

Forest bathing

Japanese researchers have found that "forest bathing", or taking walks through nature, significantly increases the level of natural killer cells in the blood, which helps your immune system fight infections and tumours. They believe the fragrant aerosols in the air are responsible for this beneficial spike.

Sounds and sights

Simply listening to nature sounds and seeing beautiful scenery has been shown to induce positive emotional states. Many audio meditations include the relaxing sounds of nature, such as birdsong, or imagery to enhance their effects. (For more on sound see page 137.)

Grounding (earthing)

Emerging evidence suggests that physical contact with the negatively charged electrons in the earth can improve a multitude of physiological outcomes. These include a reduction in inflammation, pain, and stress hormones, as well as improvements to blood flow, sleep, blood sugar levels, and the regulation of your biological clock. Researchers call this phenomenon "earthing" (or grounding), and it can be experienced by walking barefoot on the earth's surface during a walking meditation (see page 144), or sitting or lying down under a tree to meditate.

NATURAL SENSATIONS

Next time you are in nature, whether it's a small urban park or a forest, consider practising a walking meditation (see page 144) or try this three-step meditation.

1. Find a comfortable position. Sit on the ground or on a bench, or stand with soft knees and your weight back towards your heels.

2. Recruit all your five senses separately. Physically **feel** the wind and air temperature on your skin. **Touch** the earth, a rock, or a tree. Take a moment to **look** all around you, including up at the sky and down to the earth. **Listen** and notice what you **hear** far away and up close. Notice the loud sounds in the foreground and more subtle sounds in the background. Take a deep breath in through your nose and notice the **aroma** of your surroundings. Feel your tongue filling your oral cavity and notice the **tastes**.

3. Experience all your senses simultaneously. Immerse yourself fully in all the layers of the moment. If your mind wanders, return to any of the senses individually. Some call this getting in touch with your intuition and inner wisdom. What wisdom is within you?

Spending at least two hours in nature weekly is associated with good health outcomes and wellbeing.

Any kind of green space – even an urban balcony – can enhance meditation practice.

Mindful gardening

Gardening has been shown to be beneficial for your mental health, reducing anxiety and depression, lifting your mood, enhancing cognitive function and memory, and providing a greater sense of purpose and satisfaction.

Gardening intimately connects you with the natural world, and all its benefits. It can also be a great form of physical exercise when you mindfully move within your comfort zone. The good news is that if you have health conditions, including injuries or arthritis, you can modify your gardening to suit your needs.

Meditation in the garden

To enhance your gardening experience, incorporate the seven foundational attitudes of mindfulness shared by researcher Jon Kabat-Zinn. You can infuse these attitudes into any action you do, but they fit perfectly into gardening (see opposite).

Raised beds are ideal for accessibility.

Wear sunscreen and a hat to protect you from the sun.

Use good body mechanics when gardening, such as hingeing from the hips and knees, rather than rounding your back.

1
Non-judging

Notice attractions (flowers) and aversions (weeds). Can you see all equally without labelling them as good, bad, right, or wrong? Notice your self-talk around your gardening skills and shift from judgement to kindness.

2
Patience

Cultivate patience as you tend your garden, understanding that growth takes time, both in plants and within yourself. As you squat and bend, you may need to be patient with your body rather than getting caught up in frustration with its natural limitations.

3
Beginner's mind

Approach each day of gardening as if it were your first. Adopt a child-like curiosity by observing seeds sprout with fascination, getting your hands dirty, inspecting insects with wonder, and allowing yourself to marvel at the miracle of life.

4
Trust

Develop trust in your own inner wisdom and that of nature, allowing plants to thrive in their own time.

5
Non-striving

Let go of an urge to constantly seek perfection or a specific vision in your garden, embracing the beauty of the present moment.

6
Acceptance

Accept what is, even if it's not what you expected. Welcome cycles of growth, decay, and rebirth while understanding that some plants may thrive while others struggle.

7
Letting go

Recognize that some aspects of gardening are out of your control, including the weather and the will of Mother Nature.

SEVEN PRINCIPLES OF MINDFUL GARDENING

Choose one as a daily theme and observe its presence as you're gardening – or even while watering and nurturing your house plants.

Meditation and sports performance

Mindfulness enhances exercise and sports by elevating performance, enjoyment, and overall experience. Emerging research highlights its benefits in sports psychology as a way to cultivate mental clarity, focus, and a healthy relationship with competition.

Techniques like visualization aid flexibility, strength, and recovery, while mindfulness gets you in the right mindset to play. And an attitude of wu wei – a qi gong concept that translates as "effortless action" (see page 164) – can ironically improve sports performance. Wu wei involves relinquishing control and allowing things to occur naturally. By playing a sport mindfully, athletes let go of their attachment to results and enter a flow state, facilitating peak performance. Plus, non-striving takes the pressure off and supports athletes' wellbeing.

Mindful moves

Infusing mindfulness into your movement helps prevent injury, recruit muscles efficiently, and integrate a playful curiosity. Here are some examples of how you can bring meditation into your swimming, workouts, and more:

• **Swimming:** Stay present by counting strokes. Focus on how the water feels on your skin. Notice how your hands move through the water.
• **Hiking:** Immerse yourself in your senses to connect more deeply with nature and enhance your enjoyment (see page 153).
• **Team sport:** Practise non-judgement, which can elevate communication and empathy.
• **Yoga:** In a plank, for example, consider counting breaths rather than seconds to become more mindful of your breathing.
• **At the gym:** Visualize performing at your physical best (or beyond your capabilities) and your muscles getting stronger, which research suggests can boost performance.

PRE-GAME PRESENCE

Before play begins, rather than focusing on your desire to win, prioritize being present in the game.

1. Stand tall and reflect on what you enjoy most about the game. Why do you play?

2. Visualize performing at your best with joy, allowing a smile to emerge.

3. Bring a whisper sound to your breath and feel it in your throat. This is called the ocean breath (or ujjayi) and the whispering sensation promotes peacefulness. At the same time, it is warming and invigorating.

4. When ready, move into a dynamic warm-up, gradually increasing the intensity. By harmonizing calmness and vitality, you are now energized to play.

REFLECTIVE RECOVERY

Recovery is an important part of any exercise. Taking time to recuperate, rest, and recharge helps your muscles and your mind recover.

1. Take a moment to feel gratitude for all the things your body can do.

2. This is the time for slower, long-held stretches to cool down physically and energetically. Move mindfully while intentionally slowing down your breath.

3. End with several minutes of elongated exhales, making them about twice as long as the inhales (see page 51).

INNER LABORATORY
Monitor your heart

After physical activity, either use a smartwatch's heart-rate monitor or manually check your pulse by applying pressure with your index and middle fingers to your wrist near your palm. See what your heart rate is per minute. Now, sit down for the reflective recovery exercise above. When done, check your heart rate again.

Find balance with tai chi

Due to its recent rise in popularity, tai chi is sometimes called the "new yoga". Others call it "meditation in motion".

Considered a form of the ancient practice of qi gong (see page 164), tai chi was developed relatively recently, around 400 years ago, in China. It incorporates self-healing with defensive martial arts, and today it is practised primarily for its health-promoting benefits, which are supported by science; these include stress reduction, pain relief (such as back pain and arthritis), better sleep, and improved mental health. By methodically flowing through gentle movements, you gain the benefits of low-impact physical exercise, improve cognition as you remember a sequence, and promote a feeling of serenity.

Details such as hand positions foster focus.

Flowing martial arts movements promote balance and serenity.

Tai chi combines controlled movement with self-healing.

A balance of yin and yang

Based on emerging research, tai chi has become the gold standard, alongside physical therapy, for balance and fall prevention. The practice doesn't only improve physical balance, however; it also helps us find a balance mentally, emotionally, and beyond.

Taoist philosophy says a balance can naturally be found between yin (soft) and yang (hard). This symbolizes the duality that exists in nature and within ourselves. Tai chi helps us recognize that duality to cultivate inner strength, peace, and harmony. Notice that even in the dark, there is some light and vice versa, demonstrating how interactive these dualities in us are.

Tai chi helps us find a balance mentally, emotionally, and beyond.

Black
Yin
Soft
Dark
Moon
Night
Feminine
Valley
Passive
Nurturing
Cold
Winter

White
Yang
Hard
Light
Sun
Day
Masculine
Mountain
Active
Self-sufficient
Hot
Summer

The wu ji stance

The wu ji position is used in many tai chi forms to start and end the practice, similar to the mountain pose in yoga sequences. Legend has it that after thousands of years of intensive observation, this quintessential stance was identified as achieving the perfect alignment to facilitate the flow of energy freely through the body, creating a deep meditative state. You can practise this posture anywhere and anytime, but you may feel most balanced when practising it in nature.

WU JI FOR FLOWING ENERGY

Try this next time you take your dog to the park or watch the sunset.

1. Place your feet hip-distance apart and settle your weight back on your heels.

2. Soften your knees, sink your tailbone down, if comfortable, and drop your shoulders.

3. Allow your tongue to softly touch the roof of your mouth and imagine a string gently lifting your head.

4. Align your ears over your shoulders and keep your eyes open with a soft gaze at eye level.

5. Invite a sense of looseness and spaciousness into your joints and calmness to your mind.

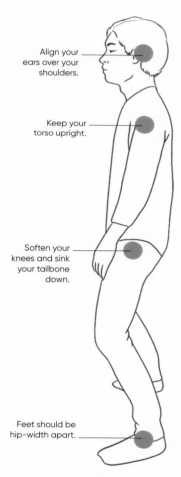

Align your ears over your shoulders.

Keep your torso upright.

Soften your knees and sink your tailbone down.

Feet should be hip-width apart.

The wu ji stance is believed to achieve the ideal alignment for energy flow.

The healing energy of qi gong

The ancient Chinese practice of qi gong can teach us a lot about body awareness and mindful movement. You can learn how to use this whenever you need a moment of calm.

Qi gong (pronounced *chee gong*) is a healing practice, which incorporates dynamic and flowing movements, static holds of poses, rhythmic breathing, chanting, and meditations designed to harness the power of qi – the vital lifeforce energy that flows within us.

Channelling energy flow

Qi gong translates from the Chinese to "lifeforce energy work". By working with your lifeforce energy through your body, you empower yourself to assist in your own healing. According to traditional Chinese medicine, there are channels in the body where qi flows, called meridians, and there are powerful areas where the qi aggregates, called dan tian. The lower dan tian, used for dan tian breathing, is just below your belly button (see right and opposite).

In this philosophy, qi should flow freely through the meridians and dan tian, and if it is stagnant, illness occurs. Attempting to feel your qi has benefits whether or not you feel it or believe in it. By shifting your awareness to the sensations and vibrations within, you will get in touch with your body's inner workings and refine your abilities to change your internal states through mindful movement, breath, and meditation techniques. You can try this at any time you need a moment of calm (see opposite).

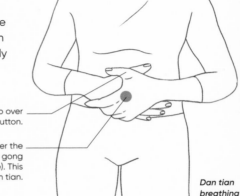

Place one thumb over your belly button.

Place your other hand over the top, stacking your lao gong points (see box opposite). This is your lower dan tian.

Dan tian breathing

Your lao gong point

The "lao gong" point is a key acupressure and acupuncture point on the palm of the hand, which is often used in qi gong practice. To find it, flex the fingers of one hand at the middle joint. The point directly below and in between the middle and ring finger is the lao gong point. Gently massage this spot on each side with the opposite hand. It is said to ease anxiety and bring balance and calm to a restless mind.

Your lao gong point sits in your palm, below your flexed fingers

The lao gong point is an acupressure point used in qi gong.

FEEL YOUR QI

This meditation can be fitted in to your day between emails or anytime you need to calm down.

1. First, establish dan tian breathing, by placing one thumb over your belly button and stacking your lao gong points on top of each other over your lower dan tian (see opposite).

2. With each inhale, feel your dan tian expand with your breath.

3. With each exhale, feel the dan tian gently contract inwards as you empty your lungs.

4. Repeat for several minutes. If you feel uncomfortable at any time, simply forget these instructions and allow your body to take over its natural way of breathing. Your body knows how to breathe, so you can simply observe.

5. Do nothing. For the next few breaths, just do nothing. This is the Taoist practice of wu wei, which can be translated as "non-doing, emptiness, inaction, or effortless action". Wu wei describes a state of going with the flow of nature, with ease rather than force. Notice how it feels to do nothing for a while. Take a few moments to just be.

Yoga for body and mind

Many find it much easier to sit still and focus in meditation after dynamically moving and stretching their bodies with yoga postures. You don't have to go to a class to do yoga – even just a few movements at the start of the day or in your lunch break can be beneficial.

When people think of yoga in the modern day, they might think of yoga classes, downward dogs, and headstands. However, physical poses are only a small part of the rich tradition of yoga. In fact, the poses are meant to prepare the body and mind to sit in meditation, which could be considered the core of the practice.

Yoga is accessible to everyone, anytime and anywhere. Short yoga breaks can be fitted in throughout your day, whether in the mornings, between meetings, to end your day, or as a wind-down stretching routine before bed. You don't need a perfect or quiet place, nor do you require any special classes or equipment. You don't even have to roll out a mat or buy any special props – a dog lead or a belt can be your yoga strap, and pillows or cushions from around the house can support your practice.

Try a tree pose (pictured opposite) in your living room or while watching your dog at the park, gentle neck stretches in the bathroom, or some simple moves in your office chair. The physical benefits of yoga include improved strength, flexibility, and balance, and relief for muscular aches and pains, but don't forget to incorporate meditation after practising some postures to optimize these benefits. The meditative benefits of yoga range from better sleep to reduced stress and increased energy.

ONE-MINUTE MEDITATION
Yoga at your desk

Practice yoga in your desk chair, incorporating the main movements of the spine. Gently round your spine, then do a seated backbend by puffing your chest forward and lifting your chin slightly. Sit tall and twist to both sides. Side bend to the right and then the left. Finally, sit still and rest in open awareness. Take a few minutes to just be.

The meditative path

The yoga tradition incorporates practical guidelines for purposeful everyday living through a system called the "eight limbs"; this can be seen as a path that emphasizes meditation practice. The limbs cover basic ethical principles for living with self-regulation, physical poses, and breathwork to prepare the body for meditation, and varying depths of meditation practice.

8

Samadhi

A higher state of being, liberated from suffering

1

Yamas

Ethical guidelines to help us develop self-control

2

Niyamas

Ethical guidelines to help us develop self-regulation

7

Dhyana

Profound state of sustained meditation

THE EIGHT LIMBS OF YOGA

These are the foundation of traditional yoga practice. When practised together, these eight limbs form a holistic approach to disciplining the mind and body.

3

Asana

Physical poses that prepare us for meditation

6

Dharana

Single-point meditation focus

5

Pratyahara

Control of the senses to turn the attention inwards

4

Pranayama

Breathwork to prepare the nervous system

MEDITATION IN YOUR YOGA SESSION

Many modern yoga classes and yoga training programmes focus mostly on physical poses and less on meditation, but you can bring meditation into any yoga that you do. Here's how to incorporate it into a class, or any practice that you do at home, to make the most of your yoga time.

1. Centre yourself to arrive in the present moment. Check in at the beginning of the practice by noticing the state of your mind and body. Is it easy or hard to be still and quiet for a couple of minutes?

2. Set an intention. What do you hope to feel or cultivate from your session? Is it to feel calmer? To still your busy mind? To relax your body? To take time out from your working day?

3. Move mindfully. As you move into a pose (asana), notice where each part of your body is. As you move, bring that presence into the transitions between poses.

4. Become aware of your breathing (breathing practices) into your session, especially at the end. Are you holding your breath? Are you aware of any tension? Notice if your breathing becomes more relaxed or deepens during your yoga session. You might like to try some of the breathing techniques explained in the book, too, such as bee breath (page 113) and alternate nostril breathing (page 68).

5. Meditate at the end of the session. Take time at the end of your yoga session to be still and meditate. Resist the urge to rush off to the rest of your day, or back to your desk, after mindfully moving your body. Notice if sitting in stillness is easier for you now. And if sitting isn't comfortable, you may want to try the lying-down practice of yoga nidra on the next page.

Before you practise

Set an intention for today. Why are you practising? Set a simple aim in the present tense and affirmative. Examples include:

- *I am taking this time to rest and rejuvenate.*
- *I am inviting ease and healing.*
- *I am listening to the wisdom in my body.*

Yoga for deep rest

A practice loved by beginners and long-term meditators alike, yoga nidra provides deep relaxation. Nidra means "sleep", but even though you are lying down and it looks like you are asleep and unconscious, you are actually awake and functioning at a higher level of consciousness.

In this state your body restores its natural rhythms and internal balance. You may even enter delta-wave brain frequencies, which are typically only seen during sleep.

Studies suggest yoga nidra could help people dealing with many concerns, including pain, insomnia, hormonal imbalances, trauma, depression, and anxiety. Research has shown that yoga nidra can increase dopamine by 65 per cent, which improves mood and modulates pain.

HOW TO DO YOGA NIDRA

Experience the benefits of yoga nidra in this 20–30-minute practice. You can read the steps now and guide yourself through it, but it may be best to have a friend read them to you or listen to the free recordings at www. meditionfortherealworld.com/nidra

1. Get as comfortable as possible. You could be lying on your back in bed, on a sofa, or in a recliner. Use cushions and an eye mask as needed for comfort. Grab a blanket for warmth since body temperature tends to drop in this sleep-like state.

2. Settle in. Welcome whatever is happening, from the sounds to the temperature of the air on your skin. Welcome all parts of yourself.

3. Affirm a deeper desire or purpose (also called sankalpa) — perhaps something personal comes to mind, or simply affirm, "I am peace."

4. Repeat your intention for practising today three times (or simply affirm, "I am taking this time to rest and reset"). Follow your intuition and trust that whatever you chose is what you need today.

5. Visualize a place where you feel at ease. It could be home, a beach, a favourite room. Go to this internal oasis with your imagination and notice how you feel. Recognize that this safe haven is always there in your mind when you need it.

6. Do a body scan. Moving from head to toe, focus on each body part for a few seconds. Start at the crown of your head, then feel the sensations in your face, neck, shoulders, all the way down to your toes. Focus on the back of your body, then the front. Focus on the outside of your body, then the inside. Feel your whole body at once. Do any areas draw your attention?

7. Feel your breath. Feel the three-dimensional movement of your body from your breath. If needed, imagine sending healing energy from your breath to any body parts that need extra love.

8. Count your breath backwards from 20. Inhale and exhale, that's 20. Inhale and exhale, that's 19... Count until you get to one, and if you lose count, start over again at 20.

9. Witness this state. Notice any spontaneous thoughts, emotions, attractions, or aversions that arise. Recognize that this is natural and part of the process, so just notice.

10. Play with opposites. If anything strong arises (like pain, agitation, coldness, tightness...), notice how it feels in your body. Where do you feel it? What would the opposite of that be? You may choose a word that represents it (such as ease or warmth). Where do you feel that in your body? What does it feel like to invite this opposite? Envision going back and forth between opposite sensations. Then invite both at once. There is no right or wrong way to do this; just play with it.

11. Let go of any effort. Allow your mind to rest in a sense of expansive, spacious awareness.

12. Awaken. Hear the sounds of your breath and then other sounds around you. Become more aware of your environment. Slowly bring movements into your body and take your time to transition back to waking life. Remember the intention you set at the beginning of the practice and bring it with you through your day.

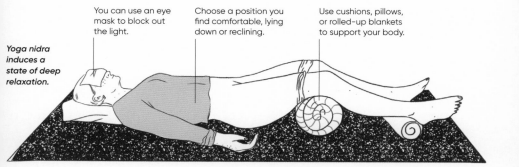

You can use an eye mask to block out the light.

Choose a position you find comfortable, lying down or reclining.

Use cushions, pillows, or rolled-up blankets to support your body.

Yoga nidra induces a state of deep relaxation.

Dance and be free

Nothing feels freer than dancing around your kitchen when no one's watching. Dance, usually in motion to music, may feel like the opposite of meditation, which is often practised in stillness and silence. However, dance pairs very well with meditation.

Sometimes it feels agitating to sit still for a formal meditation. Instead, you might feel like you want to move, or to dance. We know that music can help us get into a relaxed, meditative state, and harnessed with movement it can make you feel so much better.

Throughout the ages and in many cultures, dancing has been used to create a meditative state for ceremonies and rituals. It is effective because it integrates self-expression and an element of play. Dance is also used in many therapeutic settings, to help improve mental health, cognition, and balance.

How dance becomes meditative

Dance can particularly evoke a phenomenon called kinaesthetic empathy. Being kinaesthetic relates to your awareness of your body parts and your sensory perception of their movement. When moving with others in a partnered or group dance, the synchronization of rhythms connects us, and even something as simple as clapping on the beat in unison is a kind of dance that creates social bonds. The moment you connect with a dance partner by locking eyes or touching hands, set an intention to be present with that person. Affirm: "I am fully present with them."

A great dance to the perfect song brings you into a flow state with complete immersion in the moment. Even when simply watching others dance, your mirror neurons activate, kinaesthetic empathy kicks in, and emotions are evoked.

How your body reacts

Dance enhances your perceptions. Exteroception is your perception of the external environment – such as the sounds of the music, your sense of sight as you look around your space, and your sense of touch from your feet on the ground to the graze or embrace of another dancer. Your body also sends a steady stream of internal messages that you process through interoception (see page 142) – such as feeling your heart beating faster as the tempo speeds up.

Inputs from exteroception and interoception inform an instinctual sense called "neuroception", which is your unconscious detection of safety or threat in an environment. Creating a sense of safety is very important in dance to prevent injury, pain, or trauma triggers (see page 60). Setting healthy boundaries when dancing with others can empower us to connect while still respecting our needs. Remember that it is OK to say "no, thank you" or to stop dancing if you feel unsafe in any way. Affirm: "I respect my boundaries and those of others."

Spontaneity and playfulness

Play isn't just for children. The spontaneous nature of play brings a sense of presence (and presence often brings playfulness). Embrace playfulness whether you are partner dancing, as in a tango, or practising more free-form movement, like ecstatic dance or a solo improv in your living room.

Being playful may influence your vagus nerve, blending the activity of your ventral vagus (which supports social engagement) and your sympathetic nervous system (which energizes you). This chemical cocktail blends "feel-good" hormones with small amounts of stress hormones, making you both connected and alert. This state sets the stage for learning, processing emotions, and personal growth.

A great dance brings you into a flow state with complete immersion in the moment.

AN EASY DANCE MEDITATION

Choose some music that appeals to you – is it slow and calming, or lively and energetic? Make sure you have plenty of space, so your body can move in a way that feels enjoyable.

1. Set an intention to listen to your body and respect its limits. Affirm: "I am present and listening."

2. Take several slow breaths, bringing your awareness to your body. What signals is your body sending you now? Do you feel stressed, happy, relaxed?

3. Notice any areas that magnetize your attention. Deepen your breath and begin to move mindfully to the music, starting with any area of your body that seems to be asking for movement.

4. Orient yourself within your space by looking and listening.

5. Begin to dance. Move freely, letting your body fill the space in any way that feels good to you. Dance for one track, or for longer, if you like. When you finish, notice how you feel now.

WATCHING DANCE

You may prefer going to watch professional dancers, rather than dancing yourself. That can also be a meditative experience. Next time you watch dance, immerse yourself in meditation with these cues:

1. Sit or stand tall, becoming aware of your body positioning.

2. Tune in to the music or other sounds present.

3. Watch with empathy. Even if you are still, you may visualize yourself moving effortlessly with the dancers.

4. Observe how your breath changes.

5. Notice the ebb and flow of your emotions tied with physical feelings.

6. When your mind wanders, notice where it tends to go and return to the broad awareness of taking in the whole experience.

Art as meditation

Whether you like to colour, paint, knit, craft, play piano, or write poetry, you are an artist. You may already be aware of the feelings of relaxation and flow when engaged in creative pursuits, so let's look at how and why this happens.

Humans are wired for art. Johns Hopkins University collaborated with a multidisciplinary group of leading scientists and artists in the field of neuroaesthetics (more colloquially called "neuroarts"). They gathered robust evidence revealing how art transforms our brains and bodies. For example, in childhood, the arts have been shown to enrich social, emotional, and cognitive learning, while promoting brain development. The performing arts and music broaden our perspective, which develops empathy.

Throughout our lifespan, music improves immunity, strengthens the heart, and enhances mental wellbeing. In patients with dementia, both singing and listening to music have been shown to profoundly improve memory, cognition, and mood. In short, art in all forms helps people of all ages thrive.

Think you aren't creative or artistic? Your mode of expression could be cooking, gardening, interior design, DIY projects, or anything you enjoy. Research has shown that just a 45-minute art session could reduce the stress hormone cortisol, regardless of your skill level. Yes, even creating what you might consider "bad art" is good for your health! Plus, through mindfulness, you can appreciate art even more and approach everyday life with an aesthetic mindset.

Art for wellbeing

Spending time in an art gallery has been shown to have benefits to your mental wellbeing. It can also be a "mindful mirror" to understand oneself. Leading medical schools at Yale, Columbia, and Harvard universities integrated art museum visits into the curriculum for trainee doctors. The idea was to encourage empathetic communication, mindfulness, and self-care in the students.

OBSERVING VISUAL ARTS

Next time you are in an art gallery, or sculpture park, try this meditation, using the artwork as your focus. You can also try this at home, with a favourite piece of art – by your child, yourself, or any that you like. If you are in a gallery, resist the urge to read the label, which might direct your thoughts, and stay with your own impression.

1. Notice initial judgements, such as a tendency to label the work as good or bad art. See if you can approach it with an open and curious mind.

2. Look at it from different angles. Try observing from far away, up close to see the details, and then far away again to take it all in.

3. Notice your bodily sensations and visceral reactions.

4. Note your natural breath. Some artworks can literally take your breath away. Regulate and slow the breath to inspire greater awareness.

Create without judgement

You can enjoy the benefits of creating art without having to be amazing at it. If you haven't tried painting, drawing, or craft since school, that doesn't matter. You can try colouring, doodling, art books, craft kits – anything that appeals to you. The important thing is to give yourself time to try the activity and become absorbed in it. Let go of any idea that it needs to be "good". The purpose is in the doing with a child-like presence.

Create without attachment

Traditionally, Tibetan monks meditatively create intricate sand art called mandalas. After days or weeks of work, they destroy it. Ceremonially, they scatter the sand through nature to acknowledge the impermanence of all material things. You, too, can embrace the present moment by creating without attachment – perhaps by playing with LEGO, making a sandcastle, doodling on scrap paper, riffing on the guitar, or doing an improv dance (see page 174). These experiences can be meditative, enhancing focus.

Meditative writing

Expressive writing – recording your thoughts and feelings when overwhelmed, for example, or perhaps some form of creative writing – has been shown to help process stress. Specific techniques such as gratitude journalling can also improve satisfaction and act as a preventative measure against depression and anxiety. Experience the gratitude practices for life challenges on page 87 and express yourself with the meditative journalling exercise here.

Research suggests that aimless doodling while listening to information can improve memory recall by 29 per cent.

The act of taking a pen to paper, and letting your mind go where it needs to can be very therapeutic. Choose a pen that appeals to you and flows well. You can write in a journal or use a piece of paper.

1. Set a timer for three minutes. Sit tall and imagine a shimmering light of any colour you prefer radiating from the centre of your body. With the next few breaths, imagine that light expanding to fill your body. Then slowly expanding beyond to fill the room. Then filling the building or area. Then filling the town, country, Earth... Then expanding as far as you can imagine. You can close your eyes as you envision light gradually spreading until the timer goes off.

2. Set the timer for another three minutes. Put your pen to paper and just write. If words don't come, keep your pen on the paper and doodle until words or a drawing come. It doesn't matter what it looks like – there are no bad ideas.

3. Repeat, alternating between steps 1 and 2 several times until you feel you are done or you are inspired to write, draw, or create.

4. When you are done, you can keep your work or tear it up as a reflection of the impermanence of all things. There is benefit in the very act of creating – you don't have to keep everything.

Glossary

Acupressure points – from the Chinese Medicine perspective, these energetic points through the body can be accessed for healing by pressing or massaging them.
Amygdala – the fear centre, part of the emotional system of the brain.
Asana – the physical poses in yoga that prepare your body and mind for meditation practice.
Attention – a more focused way of consciously observing. Usually, your attention will be directed in meditation to one thing in particular, like your breath or sensations.
Awareness – a broader way of observing. In meditation, you may be directed to consciously take in many stimuli (including thoughts, emotions, sounds, etc.) around you in "open awareness" or "open monitoring".

Binaural beats – an auditory phenomenon that occurs when two tones with slightly different frequencies are listened to separately through each ear. The brain interprets these two tones as a single oscillating tone. The frequency of this oscillation, or beat, is equal to the difference in hertz (Hz) between the frequencies of the two tones.
Breathwork – breathing techniques used to induce specific outcomes.

Catastrophize – when the mind creates a catastrophe out of a real or imagined event.

Diaphragm – the respiratory muscle that separates the thoracic and abdominal cavities.
Diaphragmatic breathing (belly breathing) – the rhythmic movement of the diaphragm with each breath, which moves the belly.

Earthing – (see Grounding)
EEG – electroencephalogram, an instrument that records brain activity.

Flare – when pain or disease symptoms intensify; often brought on by stress or other triggers.
Flow state – a state of mind when a person is totally immersed in an activity.

Grounding – called earthing by researchers, this involves being in physical contact with the earth (dirt, sand, stone, wood, etc.), resulting in physiological benefits.

Heart rate variability – measures the amount of time between heartbeats, which fluctuates. Higher heart rate variability indicates resiliency and is often seen in younger people, healthier people, and athletes.

Insulin sensitivity – refers to how responsive your cells are to insulin, which is a good thing. Improving it helps reduce insulin resistance and the risk of many diseases, including diabetes.
Interoception – the process of sensing signals from inside your body, such as your heartbeat, digestion, blood pumping, etc.

Lymph – a fluid in the lymphatic system that moves through the body to filter waste.

Mantra – a word or sound that is repeated for meditation.
Meditation – the practice of focusing your attention and awareness on the present moment in a relaxed way, to promote clarity and emotional stability.
Meditative – when something is relaxing or has a meditation-like quality.

Mindful – being present with whatever you are doing, such as mindful eating, mindful movement, or mindful cleaning.
Mindfulness meditation – a formal practice, often done sitting, of being present.

Neuron – a nerve cell; conductive tissue in the body that sends electrical signals.
Neurotransmitters – chemical messengers between nerve cells to help them communicate.

Parasympathetic nervous system – the part of the nervous system responsible for relaxation and recovery, often called "rest and digest".
Prana – a term used in yoga to describe vital lifeforce energy (similar to the term qi).
Pranayama – breathing practices in the yoga system that prepare your body and mind for meditation or achieve specific states (like calm or energy).

Qi – a term from China that means vital lifeforce energy (similar to the term prana).

Relaxation response – a term coined by Herbert Benson that is the opposite of the "stress response". The relaxation response involves lowering the heart rate and blood pressure, and other calming effects.

Sound frequency – a measurement of how fast a sound wave vibrates that is measured in hertz (Hz), which indicates the number of periods or cycles per second.
Sound wave – a periodic signal that makes the air vibrate back and forth.
Sympathetic nervous system – the part of the nervous system

responsible for handling stress, often called "fight, flight, or freeze".

Triggers – a term used to describe something that brings about emotional or physical upset. Stress or lack of sleep, for example, could trigger trauma, pain, or chronic disease symptoms.

Vagal tone – the activity of the vagus nerve. Increased vagal tone is generally associated with lower heart rate and increased heart rate variability.

Vagus nerve – tenth cranial nerve; a complex nerve that extends to many vital organs and is involved in the parasympathetic response. polyvagal theory, proposed by Stephen Porges, describes two parts: dorsal (involved in immobilization and shutting down) and ventral (see right).

Ventral vagus – more specifically ventral vagal complex or circuit, the proposed branch of the vagus nerve from polyvagal theory. It supports a feeling of safety and social connection.

Yoga – a systematic way of living from India that incorporates meditation, poses, breathing practices, philosophy, and more.

Bibliography

For the most up-to-date research guide with hyperlinks to the studies for your convenience, go to **www.meditationfortherealworld.com/research**

Chapter 1

16–17 T. Sparby, "Defining meditation: Foundations for an activity-based phenomenological classification system", *Frontiers in Psychology*, 12 (2022).

19 T. Whitfield, et al., "The effect of mindfulness-based programs on cognitive function in adults: A systematic review and meta-analysis", *Neuropsychology Review*, 32(3), (2022), 667–702; J. Wielgosz, et al., "Mindfulness meditation and psychopathology", *Annual Review Clinical Psychology*, 15, (2019), 285–316; For healthy heart, see citations for pages **111–113**. For performance, see page **159**. For creativity, see page **92**.

20–21 B. Fredborg, et al., "Mindfulness and autonomous sensory meridian response (ASMR)", PeerJ, 6 (2018), e5414; P. Lush, et al., "Metacognition of intentions in mindfulness and hypnosis", *Neuroscience of Consciousness*, 2016(1), (2016); A. Newberg, brain scans found here: **www.andrewnewberg.com/research**; S. Pandi-Perumal, et al., "The origin and clinical relevance of yoga nidra", *Sleep and Vigilance*, 6(1), (2022), 61–84; G. Penazzi, et al., "Direct comparisons between hypnosis and meditation: A mini-review", *Frontiers in Psychology*, 13 (2022), 958185; R. Semmens-Wheeler, et al., "The contrasting role of higher order awareness in hypnosis and meditation", *Journal of Mind-Body Regulation*, 2 (2012); I. Wickramasekera, et al., "Hypnotic-like aspects of the Tibetan tradition of dzogchen meditation", *International Journal of Clinical and Experimental Hypnosis*, 68(2), (2020), 200–213.

22–23 Arianna Huffington: www.highexistence.com/arianna-huffington-interview; Elizabeth Gilbert: **www.thecut.com/2019/05/elizabeth-gilbert-city-of-girls.html**; Marie Forleo: **www.youtube comwatch?v=PM19QxpA7K4&feature=youtu.be**; T. Ferriss, *Tools of Titans: The Tactics, Routines, and Habits of Billionaires, Icons, and World-class Performers* (Vermilion, 2016).

24 A. Lam, et al., "Effects of five-minute mindfulness meditation on mental health care professionals", *Journal of Psychology and Clinical Psychiatry*, 2(3), (2015).

28–29 Habit pairing, called habit stacking by James Clear, or habit anchoring by Stanford researcher B.J. Fogg, PhD. James Clear quote from: **https://jamesclear.com/new-habit**.

30–31 O. Perl, et al., "Human non-olfactory cognition phase-locked with inhalation", *Nature Human Behavior*, 3 (2019), 501–512; M. Russo, et al., "The physiological effects of slow breathing in the healthy human", *Breathe*, 13(4), (2017), 298–309; P. Steffen, et al., "Integrating breathing techniques into psychotherapy to improve HRV: Which approach is best?" *Frontiers in Psychology*, 12 (2021), 624254; P. Steffen, et al., "How to breathe to improve HRV: Low and slow breathing improves HRV more than deep breathing except when using a pacer", (2022). Not yet published – available online; G. Yadav, et al., "Deep breathing practice facilitates retention of newly learned motor skills", *Scientific Reports*, 6 (2016), 37069; A. Zaccaro, et al., "How breath-control can change your life: A systematic review on psycho-physiological correlates of slow breathing", *Frontiers in Human Neuroscience*, 2(353), (2018).

33 S. Lazar, et al., "Meditation experience is associated with increased cortical thickness", *Neuroreport*, 16(17), (2005), 1893–1897.

34–35 S. Hashizume, et al., "Mindfulness intervention improves cognitive function in older adults by enhancing the level of miRNA-29c in neuron-derived extracellular vesicles", *Scientific Reports*, 11(1), (2021), 21848; B. Hölzel, et al., "Mindfulness practice leads to increases in regional brain gray matter density", *Psychiatry Research*, 191(1), (2011), 36–43; K. Fox, et al., "Is meditation associated with altered brain structure? A systematic review and meta-analysis of morphometric neuroimaging in meditation practitioners", *Neuroscience and Biobehavioral Reviews*, 43 (2014), 48–73; S. Sikkes, et al., "Toward a theory-based specification of non-pharmacological treatments in aging and dementia: Focused reviews and methodological recommendations", *Alzheimer's & Dementia*, 17(2), (2021), 255–270.

36–37 R. Chaix, et al., "Epigenetic clock analysis in long-term meditators", *Psychoneuroendocrinology*, 85 (2017), 210–214; Q. Conklin, et al. "Meditation, stress processes, and telomere biology", *Current Opinion in Psychology*, 28 (2019), 92–101; E. Epel, et al., "Can meditation slow rate of cellular aging? Cognitive stress, mindfulness, and telomeres", *Annals of the New York Academy of Sciences*, 1172 (2009), 34–53; E. Epel, et al., "Wandering minds and aging cells", *Clinical Psychological Science*, 1(1), (2013), 75–83; K. Le Nguyen, et al., "Loving-kindness meditation slows biological aging in novices: Evidence from a 12-week randomized controlled trial", *Psychoneuroendocrinology*, 108 (2019), 20–27; J. Lin, et al., "Stress and telomere shortening: Insights from cellular mechanisms", *Ageing Research Reviews*, 73 (2022), 101507; M. Mosing, et al., "Genetic influences on life span and its relationship to personality: A 16-year follow-up study of a sample of aging twins", *Psychosomatic Medicine*, 74(1), (2012), 16–22; G. Passarino, et al., "Human longevity: Genetics or lifestyle? It takes two to tango", Immunity & Ageing, 13(12), (2016); E. Soriano-Ayala, et al., "Promoting a healthy lifestyle through mindfulness in university students: a randomized controlled trial", *Nutrients*, 12(8), (2020), 2450.

40 P. Abhang, et al., Chapter 2: Technological Basics of EEG Recording and Operation of Apparatus, *Introduction to EEG- and Speech-Based Emotion Recognition* (Academic Press, 2016); C. Braboszcz, "Increased gamma brainwave amplitude compared to control in three different meditation traditions", *PloS One*, 12(1), (2017), e0170647; M. Kaushik, "Role of yoga and meditation as complimentary therapeutic regime for stress-related neuropsychiatric disorders: Utilization of brain waves activity as novel tool", *Journal of Evidence-Based Integrative Medicine*, 25 (2020).

41 P. Gomutbutra, "The effect of mindfulness-based intervention on brain-derived neurotrophic factor (BDNF): A systematic review and meta-analysis of controlled trials", *Frontiers in Psychology*, 11(2209), (2020); For research on all the neurochemicals, www.meditationfortherealworld.com/research.

42–43 R. Afonso, et al., "Neural correlates of meditation: A review of structural and functional MRI studies", *Frontiers in Bioscience*, 12(1), (2020), 92–115; Y.-Y. Tang, et al., "The neuroscience of mindfulness meditation", *Nature Reviews, Neuroscience*, 16(4), (2015), 213–225.

44–45 J. Brewer, et al., "Meditation experience is associated with differences in default mode network activity and connectivity", 108(50), (2011), 20254–9; S. Feruglio, et al., "The impact of mindfulness meditation on the wandering mind: A systematic review", *Neuroscience and Biobehavioral Reviews*, 131 (2021), 313–330; H. Jazaieri, et al., "A wandering mind is a less caring mind", *Journal of Positive Psychology*, 11(1), (2015), 37–50; M. Killingsworth, et al., "A wandering mind is an unhappy mind", *Science*, 330(6006), (2010), 932; M. Raichle, et al., "Appraising the brain's energy budget", *Proceedings of the National Academy of Sciences of the United States of America*, 99(16), (2002); A. Yamaoka, et al., "Mind wandering in creative problem-solving: Relationships with divergent thinking and mental health", *PloS One*, 15(4), (2020), e0231946.

46–47 D. Campos, et al., "Meditation and happiness: Mindfulness and self-compassion may mediate the meditation–happiness relationship", *Personality and Individual Differences*, 93 (2016); E. Epel, et al., "Wandering minds and aging cells", *Clinical Psychological Science*, 1(1), (2013), 75–83; T. Brandmeyer, et al., "Meditation and the wandering mind: A theoretical framework of underlying neurocognitive mechanisms", *Perspectives on Psychological Science*, 16(1), (2021), 39-66.

Chapter 2

50 R. Gerritsen, et al., "Breath of life: The respiratory vagal stimulation model of contemplative activity", *Frontiers in Human Neuroscience*, 12(397), (2018); M. Soos and D. McComb, "Sinus arrhythmia", StatPearls Publishing (2022).

55 A. van der Velden, et al., "Mindfulness training changes brain dynamics during depressive rumination: A randomized controlled trial", *Biological Psychiatry*, 93(3), (2023), 233–242; Y. Álvarez-Pérez, et al., "Effectiveness of mantra-based meditation on mental health: A systematic review and meta-analysis", *International Journal of Environmental Research and Public Health*, 19(6), (2022), 3380.

58–59 H. Haller, et al., "A systematic review and meta-analysis of acceptance- and mindfulness-based interventions for DSM-5 anxiety disorders", *Scientific Reports*, 11(1), (2021), 20385; L. Salay, et al., "A midline thalamic circuit determines reactions to visual threat", *Nature*, 557(7704), (2018), 183–189; L. de Voogd, et al., "Eye-movement intervention enhances extinction via amygdala deactivation", *Journal of Neuroscience*, 38(40), (2018), 8694–8706.

60–61 S. Porges, "Polyvagal theory: A science of safety", *Frontiers in Integrative Neuroscience*, 16 (2022), 871227.

67 M. Jankowski, et al., "The role of oxytocin in cardiovascular protection", *Frontiers in Psychology*, 11 (2139), (2020).

74–75 S. Bargal, et al., "Evaluation of the effect of left nostril breathing on cardiorespiratory parameters and reaction time in young healthy individuals", *Cureus*, 14(2), (2022), e22351.

76–77 See meditationfortherealworld.com/memory

78 E. Kim, et al., "Volunteering and subsequent health and well-being in older adults", *American Journal of Preventative Medicine*, 59(2), (2021), 176–186; S. Lyubomirsky, et al., "Pursuing happiness: The architecture of sustainable change", *Review of General Psychology*, 9(2), (2005), 111–131; K. Le Nguyen, et al., "Loving-kindness meditation slows biological aging in novices: Evidence from a 12-week randomized controlled trial", *Psychoneuroendocrinology*, 108 (2019), 20–27.

80–83 J. Capaldi, et al., "Post-traumatic stress symptoms, post-traumatic growth among cancer survivors: A systematic scoping review of interventions", *Health Psychology Review* (2023); B. Chopko, et al., "Associations between mindfulness, posttraumatic stress disorder symptoms, and posttraumatic growth in police academy cadets: An exploratory study", *Journal of Traumatic Stress*, 35(5), (2022); R. Gotink, et al., "Meditation and yoga practice are associated with smaller right amygdala volume: The Rotterdam study", *Brain Imaging and Behavior*, 12(6), (2018), 1631–1639; M. Shiyko, et al., "Effects of mindfulness training on posttraumatic growth: A systematic review and meta-analysis", *Mindfulness*, 8 (2017), 848–858; X. Wen, et al., "Mindfulness, posttraumatic stress symptoms, and posttraumatic growth in aid workers: The role of self-acceptance and rumination", *Journal of Nervous and Mental Disease*, 209(3), (2021), 159–165.

85–87 S. Allen, "The Science of Gratitude" (white paper), Greater Good Science Center at UC Berkeley (2018); M. Mattson, "Hormesis defined", *Ageing Research Reviews*, 7(1), (2008), 1–7.

89–91 M. Filipe, et al., "Exploring the effects of meditation techniques used by mindfulness-based programs on the cognitive, social-emotional, and academic skills of children: A systematic review", *Frontiers in Psychology*, 12 (2021), 660650; N. Gonzalez, et al., "A systematic review of yoga and meditation for attention-deficit/hyperactivity disorder in children", *Cureus*, 15(3), (2023), e36143; G. González-Valero, et al., "Use of meditation and cognitive behavioral therapies for the treatment of stress, depression and anxiety in students. A systematic review and meta-analysis", *International Journal of Environmental Research and Public Health*, 16(22), (2019), 4394; D. Simkin, et al., "Meditation and mindfulness in clinical practice", *Child and Adolescent Psychiatric Clinics of North America*, 23(3), (2014), 487–534; L. Waters et al., "Contemplative education: A systematic, evidence-based review of the effect of meditation interventions in schools", *Educational Psychology Review*, 27 (2015), 103–134.

92–93 L. Colzato, et al., "Meditate to create: The impact of focused-attention and open-monitoring training on convergent and divergent thinking", *Frontiers in Psychology*, 3 (2012), 116.

94–95 S. Cohen, et al., "Does hugging provide stress-buffering social support? A study of susceptibility to upper respiratory infection and illness", *Psychological Science,* 26(2), (2015), 135–147; M. Doğan, et al., "The effect of laughter therapy on anxiety: A meta-analysis", *Holistic Nursing Practice*, 34(1), (2020); A. Dreisoerner, et al., "Self-soothing touch and being hugged reduce cortisol responses to stress: A randomized controlled trial on stress, physical touch, and social identity", *Comprehensive Psychoneuroendocrinology*, 8 (2021); T. Field, "Touch for socioemotional and physical well-being: A review", *Developmental Review*, 30(4), (2010), 367–383; K. Light, et al., "More frequent partner hugs and higher oxytocin levels are linked to lower blood pressure and heart rate in premenopausal women", *Biological Psychology*, 69(1), (2005), 5–21; S. Shiloh, et al., "Reduction of state-anxiety by petting animals in a controlled laboratory experiment", *Anxiety, Stress, and Coping*, 16(4), (2010), 387–395; K. Stiwi, et al., "Efficacy of laughter-inducing interventions in patients with somatic or mental health problems: A systematic review and meta-analysis of randomized-controlled trials", *Complementary Therapies in Clinical Practice*, 47 (2022), 101552; A. Tejada, et al., "Physical contact and loneliness: Being touched reduces perceptions of loneliness", *Adaptive Human Behavior and Physiology*, 6(3), (2020), 292–306; C. van der Wal, et al., "Laughter-inducing therapies: Systematic review and meta-analysis", *Social Science & Medicine*, 232 (2019), 473–488; J. Yim, "Therapeutic benefits of laughter in mental health: A theoretical review", *Tohoku Journal of Experimental Medicine*, 239(3), (2016), 243–249.

Chapter 3

98–99 N. Kılıç, et al., "The effect of progressive muscle relaxation on sleep quality and fatigue in patients with rheumatoid arthritis: A randomized controlled trial", *International Journal of Nursing Practice*, 29(2), (2021). Advance online publication; H. Rusch, et al., "The effect of mindfulness meditation on sleep quality: A systematic review and meta-analysis of randomized controlled trials", *Annals of the New York Academy of Sciences*, 1445(1), (2019), 5–16; K. Simon, et al., "Progressive muscle relaxation increases slow-wave

sleep during a daytime nap", *Journal of Sleep Research*, 31(5), (2022), e13574.

104–106 B. Barrett, et al., "Meditation or exercise for preventing acute respiratory infection (MEPARI-2): A randomized controlled trial", *PloS One*, 13(6), (2018); M. Bellosta-Batalla, et al., "Increased salivary IgA response as an indicator of immunocompetence after a mindfulness and self-compassion-based intervention", *Mindfulness*, 9(3), (2017), 1–9; G. Rein, et al., "The physiological and psychological effects of compassion and anger", *Journal of Advancement in Medicine*, 8(2), (1995), 87–105.

107–109 B. Barrett, et al., "Meditation or exercise for preventing acute respiratory infection: A randomized controlled trial", *Annals of Family Medicine*, 10(4), (2012), 337–346; D. Black, et al., "Mindfulness meditation and the immune system: A systematic review of randomized controlled trials", *Annals of the New York Academy of Sciences*, 1373(1), (2016), 13–24; J. Hadaya and P. Benharash, "Prone positioning for acute respiratory distress syndrome (ARDS)", *JAMA Patient Page*, 324(13), (2020), 1361; D. Hofmann, et al., "Acupressure in management of postoperative nausea and vomiting in high-risk ambulatory surgical patients", *Journal of Perianesthesia Nursing*, 32(4), (2017), 271–278; A. Lee, et al., "Stimulation of the wrist acupuncture point P6 for preventing postoperative nausea and vomiting", *Cochrane Database of Systematic Reviews*, 2015(11), (2009).

111–113 H. Benson, et al., "The relaxation response", *Psychiatry*, 37(1), (1974), 37–46; C. Conversano, et al., "Is mindfulness-based stress reduction effective for people with hypertension? A systematic review and meta-analysis of 30 years of evidence", *International Journal of Environmental Research and Public Health*, 18(6), (2021), 2882; N. Ghati, et al., "A randomized trial of the immediate effect of bee-humming breathing exercise on blood pressure and heart rate variability in patients with essential hypertension", *Explore*, 17(4), (2021), 312–319; B. Kalyani, et al., "Neurohemodynamic correlates of 'OM' chanting: A pilot functional magnetic resonance imaging study", *International Journal of Yoga*, 4(1), (2011), 3–6; M. Kuppusamy, et al., "Effects of *Bhramari*

Pranayama on health – a systematic review", *Journal of Traditional and Complementary Medicine*, 8(1), (2017), 11–16; K. Mills, et al., "The global epidemiology of hypertension", *Nature Reviews, Nephrology*, 16(4), (2020), 223–227; G. Levine, et al., "Meditation and cardiovascular risk reduction: A scientific statement from the American Heart Association", *Journal of the American Heart Association*, 6(10), (2017) e002218; G. Trivedi, et al., "*Bhramari pranayama* – A simple lifestyle intervention to reduce heart rate, enhance the lung function and immunity", *Journal of Ayurveda and Integrative Medicine*, 12(3), (2021), 562–564.

114–115 G. Fond, et al., "Fasting in mood disorders: Neurobiology and effectiveness. A review of the literature", *Psychiatry Research*, 209(3), (2013), 253–258; S. Sinha, et al., "Effect of 6 months of meditation on blood sugar, glycosylated hemoglobin, and insulin levels in patients of coronary artery disease", *International Journal of Yoga*, 11(2), (2018), 122–128; L. DiPietro, et al., "Three 15-min bouts of moderate postmeal walking significantly improves 24-h glycemic control in older people at risk for impaired glucose tolerance", *Diabetes Care*, 36(10), (2013), 3262–3268.

116–117 S. Breit, et al., "Vagus nerve as modulator of the brain–gut axis in psychiatric and inflammatory disorders", *Frontiers in Psychiatry*, 9(44), (2018); A. Househam, et al., "The effects of stress and meditation on the immune system, human microbiota, and epigenetics", *Advances in Mind-Body Medicine*, 31(4), (2017), 10–25; C. Willyard, "How gut microbes could drive brain disorders", *Nature*, 590(7844), (2021), 22–25.

118–119 I. Goodale, et al., "Alleviation of premenstrual syndrome symptoms with the relaxation response", *Obstetrics and Gynecology*, 75 (1990), 649–655; M. Lustyk, et al., "Relationships among premenstrual symptom reports", *Menstrual Attitude*, 2(1), (2011), 37–48; J. Oates, "The effect of yoga on menstrual disorders: A systematic review", *Journal of Alternative and Complementary Medicine*, 23(6), (2017), 407–417.

120–121 S. Babbar, et al., "Meditation and mindfulness in pregnancy and postpartum: A review of the evidence", *Clinical Obstetrics and Gynecology*, 64(3), (2021), 661–682; A. Dhillon, et al., "Mindfulness-based interventions during pregnancy: A systematic review and meta-analysis", *Mindfulness*, 8(6), (2017), 1421–1437; Y. Li, et al., "Effect of mindfulness meditation on depression during pregnancy: A meta-analysis", *Frontiers in Psychology*, 13 (2022), 963133.

122–123 J. Carmody, et al., "Mindfulness training for coping with hot flashes: Results of a randomized trial", *Menopause*, 18(6), (2011), 611–620; H. Cramer, et al., "Yoga for menopausal symptoms – a systematic review and meta-analysis", *Maturitas*, 109 (2018), 13–25; C. Xiao, et al., "Effect of mindfulness meditation training on anxiety, depression and sleep quality in perimenopausal women", *Journal of Southern Medical University*, 39(8), (2019), 998–1002.

124–127 G. Durso, et al., "Over-the-counter relief from pains and pleasures alike: Acetaminophen blunts evaluation sensitivity to both negative and positive stimuli", *Psychological Science*, 26(6), (2015), 750–758; J. Grant, et al., "Pain sensitivity and analgesic effects of mindful states in Zen meditators: A cross-sectional study", *Psychosomatic Medicine*, 71(1), (2009), 106–114; A. Hanyu-Deutmeyer, et al., "Phantom limb pain", StatPearls Publishing (2022); J. Hudak, et al., "Endogenous theta stimulation during meditation predicts reduced opioid dosing following treatment with mindfulness-oriented recovery enhancement", *Neuropsychopharmacology*, 46 (2021), 836–843; L. May, et al., "Enhancement of meditation analgesia by opioid antagonist in experienced meditators", *Psychosomatic Medicine*, 80(9), (2018); G. Slavich, et al., "Alleviating social pain: A double-blind, randomized, placebo-controlled trial of forgiveness and acetaminophen", *Annals of Behavioral Medicine*, 53(12), (2019), 1045–1054; F. Zeidan, et al., "Brain mechanisms supporting the modulation of pain by mindfulness meditation", *Journal of Neuroscience: The Official Journal of the Society for Neuroscience*, 31(14), (2011), 5040–5048.

128–129 D. Hunter, et al., "Osteoarthritis in 2020 and beyond: A *Lancet* Commission", *Lancet*, 396(10264), (2020), 1711–1712; A. Guillot, et al., "Does motor imagery enhance stretching and flexibility?" *Journal of Sports Sciences*, 28(3), (2010),

291–298; V. Ranganathan, et al., "From mental power to muscle power – gaining strength by using the mind", *Neuropsychologia*, 42(7), (2004), 944–956.

130–131 R. Kisan, et al., "Effect of yoga on migraine: A comprehensive study using clinical profile and cardiac autonomic functions", *International Journal of Yoga*, 7(2), (2014), 126–132; A. Sprouse-Blum, et al., "Randomized controlled trial: Targeted neck cooling in the treatment of the migraine patient", *Hawai'i Journal of Medicine & Public Health*, 72(7), (2013), 237–241; A. Wachholtz, et al., "Effect of different meditation types on migraine headache medication use", *Behavioral Medicine*, 43(1), (2017), 1–8; Wells, et al., "Effectiveness of mindfulness meditation vs headache education for adults with migraine: A randomized clinical trial", *JAMA Internal Medicine* (2021).

Chapter 4

134–135 L. Severs, et al., "The psychophysiology of the sigh", *Biological Psychology*, 170 (2022), 108313; M. Balban, et al., "Brief structured respiration practices enhance mood and reduce physiological arousal", *Cell Reports*, 4(1), (2023), 100895.

137–139 L. Bernardi, et al., "Dynamic interactions between musical, cardiovascular, and cerebral rhythms in humans", *Circulation*, 119(25), (2009), 3171–3180; L. Bernardi, et al., "Effect of rosary prayer and yoga mantras on autonomic cardiovascular rhythms: Comparative study", BMJ, 323(7327), (2001), 1446–1449; S. Basu, et al., "Potential of binaural beats intervention for improving memory and attention: insights from meta-analysis and systematic review", *Psychological Research*, 87(12), (2023); B. Kalyani, et al., "Neurohemodynamic correlates of 'OM' chanting: A pilot functional magnetic resonance imaging study", *International Journal of Yoga*, 4(1), (2011), 3–6; S-Y. Lu, et al., "Spectral content (colour) of noise exposure affects work efficiency", *Noise Health*, 22(104), (2020), 19–27; N. Papalambros, et al., "Acoustic enhancement of sleep slow oscillations and concomitant memory improvement in older adults", *Frontiers in Human Neuroscience*, 11(109), (2017).

140–141 R. Bell, et al., "Dark Nature: Exploring potential benefits of nocturnal nature-based interaction for human and environmental health", *Curve* (2016); SDSS/APOGEE, "The elements of life mapped across the Milky Way", Sloan Digital Sky Survey (2017).

142–143 A. Bremner, et al., "The development of tactile perception", *Advances in Child Development and Behavior*, 52 (2017), 227–268; L. Crucianelli, et al., "The role of the skin in interoception: A neglected organ?" *Perspectives on Psychological Science*, 18(1), (2023).

144–145 A. Buffey, et al., "The acute effects of interrupting prolonged sitting time in adults with standing and light-intensity walking on biomarkers of cardiometabolic health in adults: A systematic review and meta-analysis", *Sports Medicine*, 52(8), (2022), 1765–1787; A. Chatutain, et al., "Walking meditation promotes ankle proprioception and balance performance among elderly women", *Journal of Bodywork and Movement Therapies*, 23(3), (2019), 652–657; A. Gainey, et al., "Effects of Buddhist walking meditation on glycemic control and vascular function in patients with type 2 diabetes", *Complementary Therapies in Medicine*, 26 (2016), 92–97; F-L. Lin, et al., "Two-month breathing-based walking improves anxiety, depression, dyspnoea and quality of life in chronic obstructive pulmonary disease: A randomised controlled study", *Journal of Clinical Nursing*, 28(19–20), (2019), 3632–3640; W. Mitarnun, et al., "Home-based walking meditation decreases disease severity in Parkinson's disease: A randomized controlled trial", *Journal of Integrative and Complementary Medicine*, 28(3), (2022).

149–151 C. Sevoz-Couche, et al., "Heart rate variability and slow-paced breathing: When coherence meets resonance", *Neuroscience and Biobehavioral Reviews*, 135 (2022), 104567; C. Streeter, et al., "Treatment of major depressive disorder with Iyengar yoga and coherent breathing: A randomized controlled dosing study", *Journal of Alternative and Complementary Therapies*, 23(3), (2017), 201–207.

153–155 G. Chevalier, et al., "Earthing: Health implications of reconnecting the human body to the Earth's surface electrons", *Journal of Environmental and Public Health* (2012), 291541; O-H.

Kwon, et al., "Urban green space and happiness in developed countries", *EPJ Data Science*, 10(1), (2021), 28; Q. Li, et al., "Forest bathing enhances human natural killer activity and expression of anti-cancer proteins", *International Journal of Immunopathology and Pharmacology*, 20(2), (2007), 3–8; W. Menigoz, et al., "Integrative and lifestyle medicine strategies should include earthing (grounding): Review of research evidence and clinical observations", *Explore*, 16(3), (2020), 152–160; J. Oschman, et al., "The effects of grounding (earthing) on inflammation, the immune response, wound healing, and prevention and treatment of chronic inflammatory and autoimmune diseases", *Journal of Inflammation Research* 8 (2015), 83–96; K. Sokal, et al., "Earthing the human body influences physiologic processes", *Journal of Alternative and Complementary Medicine*, 17(4), (2011), 301–308; U. Thiermann, et al., "Practice matters: Pro-environmental motivations and diet-related impact vary with meditation experience", *Frontiers in Psychology*, 11 (2020); M. White, et al., "Spending at least 120 minutes a week in nature is associated with good health and wellbeing", *Scientific Reports*, 9(7730), (2019); M. White, et al., "Associations between green/blue spaces and mental health across 18 countries", *Scientific Reports*, 11(8903), (2021).

156–157 J. Kabat-Zinn, *Mindfulness for Beginners* (Sounds True, 2006).

159 J. Hynes, et al., "Positive visualization and its effects on strength training", *Impulse* (2020); V. Ranganathan, et al., "From mental power to muscle power – gaining strength by using the mind", *Neuropsychologia*, 42(7), (2004), 944–956; H. Ying, et al., "The wu-wei alternative: Effortless action and non-striving in the context of mindfulness practice and performance in sport", *Asian Journal of Sport and Exercise Psychology*, 1(2–3), (2021), 122–132.

161–163 R. Lomas-Vega, et al., "Tai chi for risk of falls. A meta-analysis", *Journal of the American Geriatrics Society*, 65(9), (2017), 2037–2043; N. Sani, et al., "Tai chi exercise for mental and physical well-being in patients with depressive symptoms: A systematic

review and meta-analysis", *International Journal of Environmental Research and Public Health*, 20(4), (2023), 2828; G-Y. Yang, et al., "Determining the safety and effectiveness of Tai Chi: A critical overview of 210 systematic reviews of controlled clinical trials", *Systematic Reviews*, 11(260), (2022).

167–171 K. Datta, et al., "Electrophysiological evidence of local sleep during yoga nidra practice", *Frontiers in Neurology*, 13 (2022), 9107794; T. Kjaer, et al., "Increased dopamine tone during meditation-induced change of consciousness", *Cognitive Brain Research*, 13(2), (2002), 255–259; S. Pandi-Perumal, et al., "The origin and clinical relevance of yoga nidra", *Sleep and Vigilance*, 6(1), (2022), 61–84.

173–175 S. Koch, et al., "Effects of dance movement therapy and dance on health-related psychological outcomes. A meta-analysis update", *Frontiers in Psychology*, 10 (2019); K. Laird, et al., "Conscious dance: Perceived benefits and psychological well-being of participants", *Complementary Therapies in Clinical Practice*, 44 (2021), 101440; M. Van Vleet, et al., "The importance of having fun: Daily play among adults with type 1 diabetes", *Journal of Social and Personal Relationships*, 36(11–12), (2019), 3695–3710.

177–179 M.-P. Celume, et al., "How perspective-taking underlies creative thinking and the socio-emotional competency in trainings of drama pedagogy", *Campinas*, 39(7), (2022); J. Halamová, et al., "Psychological and physiological effects of emotion focused training for self-compassion and self-protection", *Research in Psychotherapy*, 22(2), (2019), 358; G. Kaimal, et al., "Reduction of cortisol levels and participants' responses following art making", *Art Therapy*, 33(2) (2016), 74–80; NeuroArts Blueprint, Johns Hopkins University, Aspen Institute (2021).

Index

Acknowledgements

Thank you so much to Mike, who has supported me since the beginning stages of brainstorming this book with DK. Watching you discover meditation while writing this book gave me a fresh perspective and sharpened my "beginner's mind", as Zen Buddhists say.

Thank you to Dr Sara Lazar for directing the neuroscience in the book and for your unique expertise on the current state of meditation research.

Thank you to the whole DK team from editorial to design and beyond for making this a reality. First, thank you to Ruth, my brilliant editor from *Science of Yoga*, for recommending me to write another book with DK. A special thank you to Becky, who has been there from the beginning alongside Zara in conceiving the title. Huge thanks to Holly, who has worked closely with me in editing. I don't know how you kept all my midnight edits so organized. You are a phenomenal editor! Of course, thanks to Izzy, Tania, the illustrator Michelle, as well as all who contributed. It takes a team.

Always thankful to my teachers and colleagues for your support: Paul Lam, Steffany Moonaz, Michael Slover, Laurie Hyland Robertson, Diana Wagner, Steffany Moonaz, Joe Molinari, Shelly Prosko, Michelle Martello, and my newest confidant Meritt Thomas. Thank you to the brilliant Heather Mason for inspiring my meditation practice and style.

And to all the people who consulted or looked over the research, including Elissa Epel, Steve Haines, Elisha Goldstein, Evangelia Alexaki, Jess Gruber, Polyvagal Institute, Deb Dana, Amber Grey, Justin Sunseri, and the Alzheimer's Research and Prevention Foundation.

About the author

Ann Swanson,

MS, LMT, C-IAYT, ERYT500, author of the internationally bestselling book *Science of Yoga*, wasn't a naturally "chill person", and meditation didn't come easily to her. Overcoming her own chronic pain and anxiety led her to India to study yoga and meditation, and then to China to explore tai chi. She went on to earn a Master of Science in Yoga Therapy from Maryland University of Integrative Health. Now, Ann blends cutting-edge research with ancient wisdom, resulting in accessible, real-world techniques.

Start meditating today with free audio practices as a companion to this book at **www.meditationfortherealworld.com**

Tag Ann on **Instagram: @scienceof.yoga**

Subscribe on **YouTube: Ann Swanson Wellness**

About the contributor

Dr Sara Lazar,

PhD, is a researcher at Harvard Medical School and Massachusetts General Hospital. The focus of Dr Lazar's research at Lazar Labs is to elucidate the neural mechanisms underlying the beneficial effects of yoga and meditation, both in clinical settings and in healthy individuals.

Her research has been covered by numerous news outlets, including TEDx, the *New York Times, USA Today*, CNN, and WebMD. She previously consulted on *Science of Yoga* and was the scientific advisor for *Meditation for the Real World*.

DK UK
Acquisitions Editor Zara Anvari, Becky Alexander
Project Editor Izzy Holton
Senior Designer Tania Gomes
Editorial Manager Ruth O'Rourke
Jacket Co-ordinator Emily Cannings
Production Editor Tony Phipps
Production Controller Stephanie McConnell
Art Director Maxine Pedliham
Publishing Director Katie Cowan

Editorial Holly Kyte
Design Mylène Mozas-Sauvignon, Hannah Moore
Illustration Michelle Mildenberg Lara

First published in Great Britain in 2024 by
Dorling Kindersley Limited
DK, One Embassy Gardens, 8 Viaduct Gardens,
London, SW11 7BW

The authorised representative in the EEA is
Dorling Kindersley Verlag GmbH. Arnulfstr. 124,
80636 Munich, Germany

10 9 8 7 6 5 4 3 2
005–338853–Jan/2024

A CIP catalogue record for this book is available from the British Library
ISBN: 978-0-2416-5269-5
Printed and bound in China

www.dk.com

This book was made with Forest
Stewardship Council ™ certified
paper - one small step in DK's
commitment to a sustainable future.
**For more information go to
www.dk.com/our-green-pledge**